THE MEANING OF THE CREED

PAPERS ON THE APOSTLES' CREED

EDITED, WITH AN INTRODUCTION, BY THE

REV. G. K. A. BELL

CHAPLAIN TO THE ARCHBISHOP OF CANTERBURY

LONDON
SOCIETY FOR PROMOTING
CHRISTIAN KNOWLEDGE
NORTHUMBERLAND AVENUE, W.C.
NEW YORK : THE MACMILLAN COMPANY
1921

First Edition (for the National Mission) . . *1917*
Reprinted *1918*
Reprinted *1921*

CONTENTS

CONTENTS

INTRODUCTION

I

The Meaning of the Creed is the title given to fourteen papers on the articles of the Apostles' Creed now collected in a single volume. These papers were printed first of all as separate tracts, under the supervising editorship of the two Regius Professors of Divinity in the Universities of Oxford and Cambridge, Dr. H. S. Holland and Dr. V. H. Stanton ; and they were issued in direct connection with the National Mission of Repentance and Hope, as part of the literature produced under its auspices. That Mission, as has been stated many times, was and is (for it is still in progress) a Mission of the Church, the aim of which is " to call the men and women of England to earnest and honest repentance of our sins and shortcomings as a nation, and to claim that in the Living Christ— in the loyal acceptance of Him as the Lord of all life, individual and social—lies the one sure Hope in the light of which the strain, the sorrows and the sacrifices of the war, and the task of renewal and reconstruction when the war is over, may be faced." But it was recognised by all who had to do both with the initiation and the general work of the Mission that to persuade men to this loyal acceptance of the Living Christ many things besides mere calling and claiming were necessary. In particular it was said that the endeavour which must lie at the root of the whole project was " the removal, if it may be, of popular misconception as to the character of the Gospel message and its relation to the daily life of ordinary men and women." It would seem therefore that the publication of a short series of tracts, or explanatory papers, by well-known theologians, designed for "ordinary men and women" without a special philosophical training and yet with their minds awake to the problems of theology and seeking for light, would be of real assistance to this end. Such is the origin of these papers, which have now been reset and bound together, and supplemented with a bibliography kindly contributed by one of the writers.

II

A word or two may perhaps be of use as to the purpose of creeds themselves, and then as to the source, so far as that is known, of the Apostles' Creed.

A great many people seem to think that creeds are an excrescence of the Christian religion ; a sort of "extra" imposed upon mankind by rigid and designing ecclesiastics. We are reproached for our " cold Christs and tangled Trinities," and the implication is that they are cold or tangled because our creeds have made them so. A creed is a fetter on thought, so the charge runs, and in the new age of freedom such fetters must go.

It is not to be denied that there is some justification for the charge, in the way in which we sometimes talk about and use the creeds. But as a matter of fact all the best Christian teachers agree that the Christian Creed, whatever its form, has a very different origin and serves a very different purpose. A creed is a personal affirmation of belief. *Credo in Deum Patrem omnipotentem*. . . . *Et in Iesum Christum Filium eius unicum*. . . . *Credo in Spiritum Sanctum*. I believe in God the Father Almighty. . . . And in Jesus Christ His only Son. . . . I believe in the Holy Ghost. But it is most important to remember that the Creed, though an affirmation, never pretended to explain the Christian faith, much less to exhaust it.

First of all it was intended to assert the historical basis of the Christian Religion. It recorded facts which had taken place in the visible world, and insisted that the Revelation which was at its centre was a Revelation in history. Such a "confession" of the chief facts of the evangelical story was very early recognised to be necessary as well in dealing with those outside the Church as in assuring those within it. Of this we have various important indications in the New Testament itself. There is, for example, the statement of St. Paul in Romans x. 10: "For with the heart man believeth unto righteousness, and with the mouth confession is made unto salvation"; and again the summary of the "words" in which he had preached the Gospel to the Corinthians: "I delivered unto you first of all that which I also received, how that Christ died for our sins according

to the Scriptures, and that He was buried, and
that He hath been raised again the third day
according to the Scriptures" (1 Cor. xv. 1–4).
There is the eunuch's confession before he was
baptised, which, whether it is authentic or not
in this particular instance of a baptism, at least
points to a very early practice connected with
baptism: "I believe that Jesus is the Son of
God" (Acts viii. 37). And there are also fragments
of primitive Christian hymns, as in 1 Timothy
iii. 16:

> "He who was manifested in the flesh,
>   Justified in the spirit,
>   Seen of angels,
>   Preached among the nations,
>   Believed on in the world,
>   Received up in glory":

in which some of the articles of the Christian belief
are summarised.

But in addition to this historical motive of the
Christian Creed, we have also to remember that,
especially with the longer creeds, a very prominent
function of the creed was its negative purpose. It
was meant to rule out particular rationalistic
explanations, and to protest against dogmatic
denials of certain things which the Christian believed to be fundamental. Thus Richard Hooker,
in discussing the Incarnation of the Son of God,
writes as follows:—

"It is not in man's ability either to express
perfectly or conceive the manner how this was
brought to pass. But the strength of our faith
is tried by those things wherein our wits and
capacities are not strong. Howbeit, because this

divine mystery is more true than plain, divers having framed the same to their own conceits and fancies are found in their expositions thereof more plain than true. Insomuch that by the space of five hundred years after Christ, the Church was almost troubled with nothing else saving only with care and travel to preserve this article from the sinister construction of heretics" (" Ecclesiastical Polity," Book V. ch. lii.).

Accordingly, in mere self-defence, the Church was bound to make certain large affirmations of its own. Those affirmations are not the Revelation, nor the complete explanation of the Revelation, but its safeguard, a protection of the Revelation against error.

III

In very early days, certainly before the end of the second century, a formal and public acknowledgment of the Christian faith was associated with the Sacrament of Baptism. In the closing verses of the first Gospel it is stated that Our Lord bade His disciples " make disciples of all nations, baptising them in the Name of the Father, and of the Son, and of the Holy Ghost " (St. Matthew xxviii. 19). It was therefore natural that the new converts, when they were made disciples and were baptised, should acknowledge their belief in the Father, and the Son, and the Holy Ghost, in whose Name they were baptised. And it is most probable that the arrangement and order of the Creed, as we have it now, was determined by this fact; the three paragraphs of the

b

Apostles' Creed and the Nicene Creed being concerned first with the Father, then with the Son, and thirdly with the Holy Ghost.

In the beginning such public acknowledgment, or Creed, would be of the simplest and shortest kind; and later certain amplifications would be added, and, as the history of the Creeds shews, these additions were always made as a precautionary or protective measure.

Of the three Creeds, commonly known as *The Apostles' Creed, The Nicene Creed* and *The Quicunque Vult,* the first is pre-eminently the Baptismal Creed. It is the shortest, and, though in its present form the latest, in substance it is the earliest of the Creeds; and it confines itself on the whole to certain simple statements of the old historical faith.

The Nicene Creed belongs to another class, the class of Conciliar Creeds. That is to say, it is the work of a great Council of the Church, taking its first shape in the Council of Nicea A.D. 325, and being approved in almost exactly its present form (though there is one important exception) by the Council of Chalcedon A.D. 451. It is more elaborate than the Apostles' Creed and adds theological interpretations to the simple and brief statements which that Creed contains. It is the Creed especially of the Eastern Church, as the *Apostles' Creed* belongs to the Western Church. But used alike in East and West, in the East in the Sacraments of Baptism and Holy Communion, in the West in the Sacrament of Holy Communion, it stands out pre-eminently as the great Creed of the Church.

The Quicunque Vult, "the Confession of our Christian faith, commonly called the Creed of *St. Athanasius,*" is quite unlike either of the other Creeds. Much has been written upon it and its origin. It will be sufficient here to say that it was probably composed in the fifth century by a writer in the south of France ; that in course of time it came to be sung as a canticle, in very much the same way as the *Te Deum ;* and that later still it was used as a Sermon or Commentary on the Baptismal Creed. The translation of the *Quicunque Vult* contained in the Book of Common Prayer, printed immediately after the Order for Evening Prayer under the heading "At Morning Prayer," is generally acknowledged to be misleading in certain particulars ; and attention may be drawn to the revised translation prepared by a Committee appointed as a result of the Lambeth Conference 1908, and published by S.P.C.K.*

It has been stated above that the *Apostles' Creed* is in substance the earliest of the three Creeds. An old legend relates that after the Ascension, on the eve of departing from one another on their several journeys, the Apostles composed the Apostles' Creed as "a standard of their future preaching," each contributing a single clause ; and at the end of the fourth century it was commonly believed that this was an accurate account of the origin of the Creed. But though this is manifestly untrue, and though the Creed is not the Apostles' Creed in the sense that it was actually composed by the Apostles, it is the Apostles' Creed in the sense that it represents what the Apostles taught,

*1910. Price 2*d.*

and contains many phrases which are found in the Apostolic writings. In its present form it is based on an old Roman Creed quoted by an Italian Presbyter, Rufinus, at the end of the fourth century, and by Marcellus, Bishop of Ancyra, fifty years earlier. The form of this old Roman Creed is as follows :—

I.   i.   I believe in God the Father almighty ;
II. ii. And in Christ Jesus His only Son our Lord,
     iii. Who was born of the Holy Spirit, from Mary the Virgin,
     iv. crucified under Pontius Pilate and buried,
     v.   the third day He rose from the dead,
     vi. He ascended into heaven,
     vii. sitteth at the right hand of the Father,
     viii. thence He shall come to judge living and dead.
III. ix. And in the Holy Ghost,
     x.   the Holy Church,
     xi. the remission of sins,
     xii. the resurrection of the flesh

This Roman Creed can itself be traced back to the middle of the second century, and possibly earlier still to the very first years of that century, *i.e.* to the generation which immediately follows the generation of the Apostles. From a comparatively early date variations and additions are to be found in the Creed, as it was used in different local churches, till finally it is to be read in exactly the form in which we are used to it, in the pages of Pirminius, a Bishop who worked in France and Germany, in the first part of the eighth century. And it is in this enlarged form that the *Apostles' Creed* has prevailed throughout the West.

THE
MEANING OF THE CREED

I

FAITH

" I believe."

THE word "faith" describes a variety of states of mind. In the language of religion it has a special meaning which depends largely upon the peculiar subject-matter of religion. Its use is not confined to this special subject-matter: it has associations with ordinary secular life, and it is well to begin with these in order to ascertain as clearly as possible its religious meaning.

If I arrive at the station of a strange town in order to visit its cathedral or other building of interest, I shall probably ask the first man I meet to point out to me the nearest way. He will be in no way surprised at being addressed by a perfect stranger: he will give me an answer, clear or obscure according to his intelligence, and I shall proceed to act upon his answer without demur.

When a man is feeling ill he usually sends for a doctor. The doctor recommends him to do a number of highly unpleasant things—to alter his diet, and break through habits which he has long indulged. The majority of men do not know enough about the state of their bodies or the conditions of health to understand why these injunctions are made; but, unless they propose to take their case into their own hands, they do as they are told.

In early years a child has little idea of the world and the right way of dealing with it. All his life is determined for him, and he exercises his own will within the very narrow circle of his surroundings. He constantly acts as others direct; even his ideas are insensibly formed and governed by those of his parents and others with whom he lives. If he breaks loose and acts upon his own responsibility he is likely to come to harm: it is his wisdom and his happiness to obey.

All these are cases of the exercise of faith, and they have one thing in common; in each case the agent wills and acts beyond the limits of his actual knowledge. If I argue with the man who tells me the way and require to have his direction proved to me, I shall be asking for something that I can best get by taking the road pointed out to me, and not otherwise: and I shall be insulting my informant by suspecting him, at any rate in appearance, of deceit. So I must go beyond the point at which I know if I am to make use of his answer. In like manner, the man who consults his physician does so because he does not, of his own knowledge, understand how to deal with his body; he does not wait to act upon the advice until he has reasoned it all out for himself. Still more, the child is called upon to act beyond the

limits of his own knowledge : he has the benefit
of his parents' knowledge and experience, and,
in many cases, is not only unaware of the reasons
for the action of his parent, but would be unable
to appreciate them if they were set out before him.

Thus, in all these cases—and the same is true
of endless others—faith implies action beyond the
limits of knowledge. And this feature has caught
the attention of the popular mind, so that it has
been wrongly assumed that the essential element
in faith is ignorance. This is a mistake which
has very unfortunate consequences. It is a
mistake, because the real ground upon which a
man acts in faith is not the fact that he is ignorant,
but the belief that the person whom he trusts
has the knowledge necessary for the occasion,
and the disposition to give others the advantage
of it. When I ask the way, I am doubtless ignorant
of the answer or I should not put the question.
But when I act on the information I receive I
do so because I believe that my informant knows,
and that he is honest and will not deceive me.
This is the positive and determining ground of
my action. It is the same in the other two cases.
I *consult* the physician because I am ignorant,
but I *act* on my faith in his knowledge and goodwill. In both these cases the occasion for the
exercise of faith is, in a sense, accidental : it
arises out of particular circumstances, and the
ignorance which starts the inquiry is a prominent
feature in the transaction. The position of the
child is different. His whole life is dependent
upon his parents, and rests upon his confidence
in them ; but here also his faith is established

upon his positive confidence in his parents, and not upon his own deficiencies. It is continually being justified and strengthened by experience, if his home is a good one, so that he is able to sustain " trials of faith " and to surmount difficulties. His faith grows as his knowledge of them grows, and survives even when his dependence has passed into independence and friendship.

It is of great importance to emphasise the positive side of faith ; to forget it and to lay stress upon the other leads to various kinds of mischief and error. Most of the misunderstandings and perversions of the idea of faith come from this mistake. Faith is always closely allied to reason ; it always, when it is right faith, assumes a rational order ; it goes beyond the point of knowledge, but it does so in the belief that the contents of knowledge and of faith will ultimately be found to be continuous and in harmony. The lack of this conviction is the most fruitful error of delusion and deception. The credulous man is he who has no conception of a rational order, or a false one, and is therefore at the mercy of any one who appeals to his imagination. Hence the prosperity of various types of quack and swindler. Their victims have no valid, general idea of the world and its order, or of the way in which commercial enterprise actually works. They desire health, or they desire riches, and they easily give in to the seduction of schemes which promise them one or the other. In a perverted sense they may be said to have faith in those who swindle them ; in truth their action is quite irrational, which faith never is ; it depends upon general ignorance, or ignorance in some special department of life, or upon some particular state of the emotional or nervous system. It is hardly necessary to point out the effect of the anxiety caused by the present war upon the veracity and the credulity of ordinarily sensible people.

Faith, then, in ordinary life is a rational process, by which the mind attains to conclusions and acts in advance of positive knowledge or logical deduction. The man so acting probably thinks that if he knew more he would obtain his conclusions by demonstration; he is prepared to act upon it in anticipation of this, because he trusts the goodwill, or the knowledge, or the combined goodwill and knowledge of some one else. This leads us to notice another common feature in the exercise of faith. It is not merely an intellectual process by which a particular result is attained, it is also an act of confidence in the character of a person. I believe what I am told, or I do what I am told because I have confidence in the person from whom I get information or commands. This element enters into all manifestations of faith, but it is obviously one which may vary greatly in degree. Personal confidence is at its lowest, though it is certainly present, when I accept the information from a casual stranger. It is most fully and comprehensively displayed in the confidence of a child in its parents. This is a confidence which not only covers a particular incident, or set of circumstances, it affects the whole life of both parties. It is on this side that we approach religious faith—the faith which rests upon God.

It is probable that there is no such effective way of understanding what faith in God means as by considering the relation of parent and child. We are not involved in the complicated question of the early history of religious ideas. For the purpose of this paper the fundamental fact of all religion—a belief in God—must be taken as our starting point. In its early stages the faith in God, like the child's faith in his parent, is inarticulate. It is rather a kind of atmosphere in which life is spent than a definite and articulate conviction. The child does not raise the question how his parents got there, or what their functions are: he takes them for granted, and, if he lives his own life to some extent, he always calls upon them for what he wants. This closely resembles an early and undeveloped stage in religion. The resemblance is not exact; there are many influences which prevent any such simple relations; but the definitely religious element, which underlies much that is only partly religious in undeveloped man, is similar to the inarticulate and unreasoned confidence of a child in its parents.

Faith in God at an elementary stage such as this is largely emotional. It is not true to say that it is mere emotion, because it has in it the aptitude for becoming articulate and being made intelligible. The growing experience of life will give it form and definiteness and elaborate its real meaning and use. Here again the growth of the individual illustrates the growth of the race. The child who at first has no clear ideas of his proper relation to his parents finds out as his experience increases what it really means. If at the early stages he has little more notion of his parents than as means to supply his wants and afford him protection, he soon comes to know something of their character. He notices their acts, and begins, sooner perhaps than they are aware, to criticise and judge them. Both sides will be perpetually revealing themselves, each to the other, and very different results may be attained; the child may grow into a love and veneration which continually strengthens, though it never really destroys his freedom and independence, or he may try his parents and find them wanting, and pursue his own life without any real help or guidance from them.

There is, at first sight, no reason why the growth of religious faith should not follow the same simple lines as these; it would seem natural that the wider experience of life should bring additional clearness and intelligence to man's faith in God, as it does to the child's faith in his parents. It is obvious that the blind and unexplained faith in God which belongs to the early stages of religion can be of no use when life itself has become difficult and complicated. Religion must have a meaning and a power in the life of civilised man as well as for the savage; it must deal with his most complicated problems, and help his ideals in his circumstances as they change, or it will drop out of use and disappear or become a mere superstition. But the process of adapting religion to new and more difficult circumstances is not a simple and easy one, and this is due to two very important facts. In the first place, man's knowledge of God is not like the child's knowledge of his parents, part of his daily experience of the world: it is obtained by indirect methods. And secondly, between God and man there stands the fact of sin. We will consider these two points in the reverse order.

Sin implies not merely the commission of certain acts which contravene the law of God: it covers also and involves a perverted attitude towards God in general. The root of it is self-assertion, the refusal to follow the guidance and obey the commands of God; and it results in weakness of will—a man cannot do the things that he would—and spiritual blindness. The sinful man loses the power of seeing even what it is within the power of his nature to see; his spiritual sense becomes dull, and the lust of the eyes, the desire of the flesh, and the pride of life take command over him. Man's development has been carried on under the shadow of this power. He has developed and advanced, but the whole process has been perverted by the presence of sin. Thus sin has never shown any sign of disappearing, however successful the advance in civilisation; new steps in civilisation have rather given occasion for the appearance of new types of sin. And it is plain from the whole history of mankind that something more is necessary to get rid of this blighting influence than the machinery which he can devise for himself. This brings us in sight of the most difficult of all the questions connected with faith. Man cannot by his own wisdom or good deeds save himself from his sin. How, then, is he to be saved? St.

Paul says by his faith. We must now ask, what does this mean, and how is it connected with the uses of the word "faith" which we have just been considering ?

We have pointed out that sin not only involves a spirit of hostility, a consciousness of broken law and of guilt, but it also blinds the spiritual sight, and prevents a man from becoming aware of the presence and love of God. On the other hand, faith, such as we have had in view above, expresses the spirit of sonship, it excludes hostility, it sustains trial and proves true. If the sinner can pass from the state of sin, with all its consequences, into the condition of sonship, he is saved from his sin ; he has passed into the favour of God ; his faith, which is the proper expression of sonship, has saved him. But can he at will produce faith ? Can he simply change his attitude towards God, as he might change his attitude towards a neighbour with whom he had a quarrel, and come into Divine favour ? It is a hard saying, especially in modern ears, but the answer of the whole Bible to this question is an emphatic No. The efforts at moral improvement in Western nations, the deep and intense aspirations of the saints of the Old Testament, the experience of the Apostles in the New Testament, are all at one in this denial ; something is wanted on God's side that will break down the barrier that holds man off from Him and make possible the faith that saves.

We noticed that the knowledge of God differs from our knowledge of one another in being indirect ; we may extend this statement by pointing out that all *certain* knowledge of God, and every trustworthy step forward in our knowledge of Him, is given to us by Him. Speculation —reflection upon nature and other such processes lead us to conclusions which we can never fully make good; our real and trustworthy knowledge of God comes by revelation. No doubt it is with God's will and under the leading of His Spirit that men feel after Him and find Him even in nature; but there is a difference between this sort of knowledge and that we call definitely revealed, and it is convenient, therefore, to retain a different name. With this caution, it is true to say that the history of Revelation is the history of the Jewish religion. And the method pursued by God in making Himself known was to act in the field of history, and declare there His Power, His Holiness and at last His Love. The process is a long one. Man is not for many centuries able to respond to the higher calls and the fuller knowledge of God, and to produce the faith that saves; he has to learn his own need as well as God's answer to it; it is not until the fulness of the time that Christ comes. It was in the loving kindness of God that He delayed all those years; it was out of His love for the world that He sent His Son. The long preparation had failed to carry all its meaning to the chosen nation; they crucified Him Whom they should have welcomed; but in this crucifixion the barrier which held man off from God was done away, and the path lay open to reconciliation and the sense of adoption. It is when man responds to this long revelation of loving care and trusts, though he cannot fully explain, the efficacy of the Death of Christ, that he produces the faith which saves. He trusts no more in his own righteousness and his own efforts at reform, and he surrenders himself wholly to the power of God, and seeks for no other salvation. It may be that he still has to struggle against survivals of evil which come to him from his past, but by his surrender to the appeal of Christ's Cross he has in him the power which will carry him through all dangers and enable him to work out in detail all that his first surrender promises.

Thus the faith in God, which is the climax of man's longing for God, appears as a true consciousness of sonship, and has, in spite of differences, many points of likeness to the faith of the child in his father. It is the fulfilment of the hope which has been astir in the mind of man wherever he has felt the presence of God in the world—the hope that he may build a bridge between himself and God, and enter into friendship with Him. That is the central meaning of faith, in religious language. To explain it in full would require a complete system of theology, and, at the least, would lead us into questions for which there is no room here. There are, however, one or two points which it is desirable to consider somewhat attentively before we leave the subject.

It cannot be stated too strongly that true faith in God is always a response to an appeal from God, and never a result of pure speculation. It is very hard for men to believe this. As they develop in knowledge of the world, as they take a wider interest in human life, they cannot fail to feel increasingly competent to raise and to solve questions. The savage, who is terrified out of his wits by a thunderstorm or an eclipse, runs to his god to escape from a world that is too many for him. It is hard for the man who knows all about thunderstorms and eclipses, who can bind to his service the strongest forces in nature, who can battle with disease, who can think out questions of science and economics and sociology—it is hard for such a man not to feel that he is equally competent to define what is and must be true of God. But the knowledge of God is not like the knowledge of a natural force or an economic law: it is the knowledge of a Person Whom we cannot see, and Who is known to us through His acts. These give us definite knowledge, but they also limit our knowledge, and we are dependent on them. And the way by which we interpret them is faith. The history of pure speculation in religious matters bears out this position. No speculative theory of the Being of God has ever succeeded in retaining a clear view of Him as a Person. We have learnt much from thinkers who have given their minds to the problems at the root of religion; and it cannot be denied that religion presents many difficulties to the mind. But the essence of religious activity is to hold communion with a Person—Whom we love, and Who loves us. We may not understand in full what we mean when we say these things of God: His nature is much more than anything we can mean by " personal," but at least we know that He is not less than personal, that at least what we mean by communion and love in our intercourse with men is true of the religious union between us and God. The notion of a remote First Cause—which is one of the results to which pure speculation is apt to lead—or that of an immanent power inseparable and indistinguishable from the world—which is another of such results—has no room for religious communion, and is at the opposite pole of thought to the faith which saves. It has lost the essential spring of religious life.

Faith in the sense in which we have been considering it has many forms. It needs no learning to attain it; like the love of a parent it is within the capacity of the simplest. But it does not necessarily stop at this level. It is, as we said, a surrender to the appeal of God, a realisation of sonship, a conviction of victory over sin in the strength of Christ. But it is a response to a revelation of Himself on the part of God, and this is a thing which has consequences. The more full the man's experience who has the faith, the more careful he is to study and reflect upon the acts in which the character of God is revealed, their history, and the method of God's government of the world, the more articulately he brings his faith into contact with all his life, so much the more will he desire or feel he has definite and trustworthy knowledge of God. He will not be content with inarticulate devotion, he will want to express his convictions and his knowledge about God in words. Within certain limits he can be sure that his expressions—if not fully adequate even to what he knows of God—are true. When faith is thus embodied in language it is called a creed. There is no reason why a creed should not be both true and permanent; it will not, as we have said, express all that is true of God, but that does not mean that any other expressions, however incompatible with it, are equally true. To say that God is our Father does not say all that is true of Him, but it is true, and any proposition that is incompatible with this is not true. There is a real sense in which the word "faith" is used as interchangeable with creed. It is true, as we have said, that a sincere faith, even if it is inarticulate, saves the sinner; but the faith which is also articulate and coherent is a more developed thing, and more fitly adapted to an advanced stage of human life. For our faith in Christ is meant to be a light to all our nature—to guide and give peace to our mind as well as our will and our spirit; if we leave it to rule our feeling only and deny it the relief of the spoken word, we introduce a division into our nature, and leave a large part of it outside the rule of Christ.

There are those, it is true, who pass beyond articulate language and even thought, and who have attained something like the heavenly vision. For them faith itself seems to have been transcended, and at times, at any rate, they seem to be free of the body and all its cumbrous methods. They are like the Apostles on the mount of Transfiguration, they do not know what to say. But most of us have to live below the mount and mix in the confusion of secular life; and those will be happiest whose faith covers most ground, and who feel its force in every district of their life.

II
GOD

" In God the Father Almighty, Maker of heaven and earth."

IN considering this greatest of all subjects, there are three inquiries which we shall make :

(1) How did we get our belief in God ?

(2) How is that belief justified to our intelligence ?

(3) Can we know God by actual experience ?

These questions will be found to cover sufficiently for our present purpose the vast discussions which, for many centuries, have occupied the minds of those who have grappled with the problem before us.

We shall not lay down any definition at the start of what we mean by the great word " God." We shall let its meaning appear as we proceed.

(1) Modern investigation of the thoughts and customs of primitive peoples has yielded much valuable material with which to supply an answer to our first question. The study of the origins of religion in all its forms, and the study of religions in relation to one another, have led to important results. Perhaps the most characteristic and universal form of the primary religious impulse is the belief expressed by the *mana* of the Melanesians,

or the *orenda* of the Hurons, a sacred mysterious potency in persons and things. To this *mana* is attributed in turn all forms of psychic energy, thought, memory, will, etc. From this root seem to spring the two main elements in primitive religion : (*a*) belief as regards the existence and influence of spirits, and (*b*) forms of ritual observance. There is uncertainty as to which of these two emerges first : but, for our purpose, it is important to observe that, so far as we know, all primitive peoples are, or tend to be, animists ; that is, believers in the existence and operation of spiritual powers. Face to face with the world, confronted with a multitude of things which are in various degrees mysterious and intractable, the savage inevitably discerns the influence of spiritual agencies which, like himself, are possessed of mind and will.

It used to be thought that the savage is a materialist. It is now known that this is absolutely false. He is always a believer in a spirit-world. Behind the things that he sees and handles he believes in the presence and operation of unseen conscious agencies. Every notable feature of the world about him, every mountain, or river, or great tree ; every striking event or influence which affects his life, such as a storm, or a disease ; every difficulty or trouble which he encounters in his contact with the material world : all are connected in some undefined way with spiritual activities which he is somehow impelled to postulate. As savage thought advances these ideas assume clearer outlines, and there emerges belief in a vast multitude of nature-spirits. In addition, primitive man has, as a rule, a profound conviction as to the continued existence of the departed. He does not think that the end of the bodily life involves also the ending of the human spirit.

Usually the spirits are regarded as malignant, or, at all events, jealous. They must be carefully remembered and considered. Their desires must be attended to. Their hostility must be guarded against. Hence follow all sorts of magical rites and observances which mimic the respect which is paid to important men. Also the terror of the spirit-world overshadows, like a black cloud, the whole of savage life. None can tell when some spirit who has been offended, by neglect or injury, may take vengeance for the affront. Life is beset with unseen perils.*

It is easy to see that we have here the origin of pagan religions very clearly indicated. As thought rises to higher levels the world of petty, spiteful spirits is replaced by a hierarchy of nature-gods, terrible or beautiful, who are regarded as possessing superhuman powers, who are more or less interested in the doings of men, and of whom therefore account must be taken in human affairs.

It has often been pointed out that underneath all polytheistic faiths may be detected a substratum of animism. And even so highly developed and philosophical a creed as Buddhism scarcely conceals the surviving animistic beliefs of the majority of its unlearned votaries. In Burma, for example, the most completely Buddhistic country in the

---

* On the origins and nature of primitive religions see E. B. Tyler, *Primitive Culture*; J. G. Frazer, *The Golden Bough*; R. R. Marett, *The Threshold of Religion*; and the works of Jevons, Lang, Tiele, etc.

world, the dominant religion is but a thin veil spread over the primitive animism.

Out of this animism there arose those religions which impressed their character on such great peoples as those of ancient Egypt, of Greece, and of India; religions which venerated gods of the sun and the moon, of earth and ocean, and which also recognised a pantheon of deities of various grades of importance and power. A wide survey of such creeds reveals the fact that any part or aspect of human experience, any department of life or quality of character, might come to be represented by a corresponding deity. The tendency of man's mind in relation to this matter is to project himself and his experiences into the unseen, and to find there the counterpart of his own spiritual nature.

We cannot therefore be surprised to find that the organisation of human society is reproduced among the gods; and as kingly rule was established over great nations and territories it became inevitable that great sovereign deities should receive recognition. Thus Zeus, Jupiter, Odin emerged. Thus also we find national and tribal gods, such as Bel and Marduk; and in the city-states, whether monarchical or republican, deities who, like Athena at Athens, represented the genius of the community.

Thus the passage from primitive animism to polytheistic forms of religion becomes easily intelligible; and polytheism, let it be noted, is, on its own level, an eminently reasonable creed. The world is full of differences and oppositions, of conflicting agencies and influences : good and evil, light and darkness, pleasure and pain, health and disease, tribe warring with tribe, community competing with community. How natural for those who start with the animistic habit of mind to regard all these contending elements as the spheres of the activity of diverse spiritual agencies ! From this point of view monotheism is a very difficult creed. How can man believe in one sole, supreme universal Deity, when the world is so full of antagonisms, and there is no apparent over-ruling unity capable of bringing them all into harmony ? Yet monotheism appeared, and achieved, within certain limits, a very wonderful victory. The Old Testament gives the record of its triumph. But it is not there only that we must seek for the history of monotheism. Greece, Persia, Chaldea, India, China, and Japan can all claim some share in this great revelation of supreme truth. In the great age of Greek thought there were minds which were able to rise to the conception of a Supreme One, a Being essentially One (μορφὴ μία) though expressed by " many names." Indian mono-theism, as recent investigations have disclosed, can be traced through a history of thousands of years.* In China and Japan, under the veil of Buddhism, Amida-worship has become the vehicle of a faith which is, in essence, a monotheistic creed. Amida, who is styled the true Buddha, is worshipped as the One Supreme Being, whose chief character is mercy, and who, through incarnation and sacrifice, accomplished man's salvation. Faith in him brings deliverance to the believer and secures

* See Grierson, art. *Bhakti-marga* in *Encyclopædia of Religion and Ethics*, and MacNicol, *Indian Theism*.

eternal happiness.* Yet it must be admitted that in all these cases monotheism is maintained with difficulty; and in India and China there is a probability of Christian influence in the later developments.

Only along the lines of that great spiritual progress recorded in the Old Testament can we find the true revelation and the definite triumph of monotheistic faith. Yet it was through hard struggle that victory came. In Israel there was, as in other ancient peoples, faith in a national God, a God Who stood for the genius and destiny of the nation. The history of Israel is the history of how the God of the nation came to be recognised as the God of the universe. It is the record of the final conflict of polytheism with the pure creed. In that conflict the prophets of Israel were the leaders. They it was who, above all, preached the true faith, denounced idolatry, and asserted the supremacy of Jehovah as the only God, over all things in heaven and earth, over nature and over history. (See *e.g.* Amos ix. 7; Isaiah ii. 5–22; xxxvii. 26–33, and in the later Isaiah, xl. 12 to end.) Out of the labours of the prophets as the interpreters of the experiences of the Hebrew race, and out of the terribly severe discipline through which that race passed, emerged an unshakable conviction in the great creed expressed by the words: "Hear, O Israel, the Lord our God is one Lord." From Israel the monotheistic faith passed to Christianity and to Islam, and so became the possession of the modern world.

There is, however, another side to this develop-

* See Arthur Lloyd, *The Creed of Half Japan.*

ment, and one which is equally important. There is a corresponding moral advance. Monotheism is essentially an ethical creed. Animism and polytheism, with their recognition of the divinity of the diverse elements in the world, whether good or evil, can never attain to a high moral level. Pantheism is in a similar position. If good and evil are alike divine, why should one be preferred to the other ? In perfect accordance with this is the fact that, among pagan peoples, religion and morality are but loosely connected. Among the ancient Greeks and Romans morality was regarded as the cement of social life. Duty to the State made men become moral heroes. When morality sought justification it found it in philosophy. In the East to-day the higher morality springs out of Buddhism and other philosophic creeds.

Monotheism unites religion with morality. So it was in the religion of Israel. So it must ever be, because if God is One, and supreme over the universe, His will and, on deeper reflection, His character, become the standard of personal life. And, with growing experience and clearer insight, the knowledge of God and the moral standard rise together. The human conscience, which in its beginnings is the mere apprehension that there is a distinction between good and evil, between right and wrong, gains enlightenment: it attains a larger grasp of the details and circumstances of life, marking out whole departments of conduct as good or evil: it acquires more and more a peculiar sensitiveness to moral differences, and, in the light of monotheistic faith, identifies all good with the whole meaning and plan of the universe, and turns from evil as that which is subversive of the universal purpose. It is monotheism which enables us to speak of conscience as the voice of God.*

Thus it is that man has been led, throughout the course of human history, from the impulse which makes him suspect and fear some spiritual agency in every remarkable thing which he encounters in the world, up to that noble faith in the One Supreme Deity which has been the light of life to nearly all the greatest of human beings during the last two thousand years.

A signal proof of the liberation and elevation which monotheism brings is found in an experience which is frequently enjoyed by Christian missionaries. When to the animistic savage there finally comes, after many a hard struggle with his hereditary ideas, the belief that God is one, holy, good, and supreme in the universe, there follows a glorious spiritual illumination. The terror of the evil spirits, that black cloud which overshadows savage life, vanishes: the man is able to look up with confidence to a Father in Heaven against Whose power no demon or magic spell can prevail.

(2) We must now turn to the very important question, How is this monotheistic faith justified to the intelligence ?

There are two classes of thinkers who dispute this creed. First, atheists deny the existence of God ; secondly, agnostics hold that the evidence given for it is so unsatisfactory and the difficulties it involves are so serious that they must pronounce a verdict of " not proven." Some go further and

---

* On the imperfection of Mahommedan Monotheism, see Jevons, *Comparative Religion*, pp. 133, 134.

say that it cannot be proved, because all the ideas involved are self-contradictory.

It is not necessary to consider atheists separately, because the arguments on which they rely are the same as those which are urged by the agnostics. The Atheist draws a more definite inference, and therein weakens his position. He tries to prove a negative—a very difficult thing to do. The Agnostic's position is much stronger. He appeals to the difficulty of solving all the ultimate problems, the impossibility of finding adequate terms to express ultimate truths, the weakness of many of the arguments which have been employed in the past, and concludes that the problem of the universe is insoluble. We can only, he holds, have real knowledge in the limited sphere which has come under our observation and been subject to experiment. Beyond this all is uncertain.

Four proofs were, in the past, mainly relied on to establish the doctrine of God's existence. The first appeals to the principle of causation. Every thing or event must have a cause. The universe, therefore, must have come from a great First Cause. It is now admitted that this proof is not sufficient, because the universe as a whole is not comparable with the things which it contains. Yet the argument is not valueless, because the material world is essentially changing, fugitive, in its nature; and even modern science points to an end of all material process when, by dissipation of energy, all creative movement shall cease. But if the world be finite in time, what caused its beginning?

The second proof argues from the wonderful adaptation of means to ends in nature, the structure of the human eye or hand, for example, so marvellously fitted for their purpose. Instances of such adaptations are to be found in countless numbers. Surely they prove a designing mind. This argument, though acutely criticised by Kant and others, was regarded as of overwhelming force until Darwin's doctrine of the origin of species pointed to a natural process by which these wonderful adaptations may have come about. According to this doctrine they are due to the slow adjustment of organism to environment through countless generations. It must be admitted that this new light of science changes the problem. But it does not destroy the argument. Instead of considering particular instances we must now consider the whole evolutionary process. When we do this we see a vast age-long procession and mark its direction. We see an order in which matter leads on to life, life to consciousness, consciousness to humanity, humanity to a highly-organised social existence in which lofty moral ideals appear, and in which a glorious vision of a perfected humanity, a Kingdom of God, emerges. Here, in this highest point of the great series, we feel justified in discerning the meaning, the purpose of the whole. The design is revealed, and it is a design which seems clearly to show a great designer.

The third proof is of a highly metaphysical character, and cannot be so easily outlined. But, even in this short paper, we hope to be able before concluding to bring out into some degree of clearness its essential nature.

A fourth ground of proof has been found in the moral nature of man. Conscience is the revelation of man's responsibility to some supreme authority. Against this can be urged those theories of the origin of moral distinctions which trace them to a purely natural source. We need not pause to discuss this question, for we have already seen how close is the connection between monotheistic faith and belief in the absolute and eternal nature of the good.

All these proofs possess, as we have seen, a real value. Yet it must be confessed that none of them provides that rigorous certainty which is demanded in mathematical demonstration or in physical science. So clearly has this element of uncertainty been recognised that some thinkers, for example Bishop Butler, have held that it is part of God's method of dealing with us to make the proofs of religion of such a nature that doubt is possible. Thus the intellect becomes a means of moral discipline. Man is put upon trial. He learns that he is responsible for the use of his intelligence. Every department of human life rests upon a moral basis.

This last consideration opens the way for another presentation of the theistic problem. It will be found that there is an underlying reason in the whole process by which man attained to his belief in God. In his life on earth man is always feeling his way. He is like a creature moving over thin ice and finding, as it goes, how far the ice will bear. So it is in science. By observation and experiment results are attained. It is found, after repeated testing and verification, that there is a certain degree of constancy in natural processes. Fire melts lead to-day: it will do so to-morrow.

You can depend upon fire to melt lead. Out of such observations the whole vast structure of science has arisen. And the more science advances the more certainly does it appear that there is an underlying trustworthiness in nature. The laws of Nature, which science discovers and codifies, are simply ways in which this constancy is expressed. Further consideration shows that the principle which thus comes to light is fundamental in all knowledge, in all use of our faculties. What is true to-day will be true to-morrow. What human power can effect to-day, human power can effect to-morrow. What man has done man can do.

Herbert Spencer, in setting forth the foundations of his agnostic creed, concludes his examination of ultimate religious ideas with these words: " The Power which the universe manifests to us is utterly inscrutable." It is an obvious criticism that this is a contradiction. If the Power is manifested, how is it utterly inscrutable ? It is surely clear that so far as it is manifested it is not utterly inscrutable. More important still is the observation that even the most extreme agnostic has to admit that the universe is the manifestation of some great power. This being so, it would seem to be more reasonable to endeavour to gather the character of that Power from the nature of the manifestation which takes place in the universe than to draw a universal conclusion of inscrutability from the fact that there are difficulties involved in the ideas and terms which men have employed in old creeds and philosophies. It would certainly be more scientific.

Does our experience warrant any conclusion

as to the character of the Ultimate Power ? It
certainly does. All our knowledge as well as the
whole structure of our ordered life depend upon
the principle that the Power which the universe
manifests to us is trustworthy. And every advance
in science is a further extension of the sphere of
this trustworthiness. Further, the great progress
which has taken place throughout the history of
human thought in the formation of the conception
of God has proceeded on lines which are exactly
parallel to this scientific advance. The animistic
savage regards the world as the scene of the operation of diverse and unaccountable spiritual powers.
For him the things and events of nature are capricious. He has no sense of order in the universe.
As thought rises, certain deities of a higher and
more consistent character seem to emerge and
dominate the others. This is polytheism. With
the appearance of monotheistic faith there comes
the conception of the world as under one great
supreme rule. Everything that happens must,
on this view, however unaccountable it may seem,
have some place in the will or purpose of the only
God. Order has taken the place of disorder.
Hence the wonderful liberation which comes to
the animistic savage when he is suddenly lifted
from the bottom to the top of the scale of religious
ideas. He has learned to think of the universe as
under one supreme rule, and that rule trustworthy.
The truth is that man's religious consciousness
has attained the goal more quickly than his
scientific consciousness. By an act of faith the
religious mind has already reached the conclusion
towards which science is still painfully striving.

When we have once gained the belief that the power which the universe manifests to us is trustworthy we have all that is necessary to establish our theistic creed. We must apply the principle which has come to light not merely to the processes and events of the material world, but also to the facts of organic life and to the moral and social life of man. We must believe that not a sparrow falls to the ground without the care of the Supreme, that no human soul is "cast as rubbish to the void," that the very hairs of our head are numbered, that moral values are no mere current coin of social existence, but are the human expression of values which in their final quality belong to the Eternal. Work out the principle of the trustworthiness of the power which the universe manifests to us to the full, and it becomes that final summing up of all that Christianity teaches as to the nature of God : " God is Love." In the moral sphere the term "love" is the only complete expression of trustworthiness. Hence the strength of the appeal which Christ's teaching of the Fatherhood of God has ever made to the human heart.

It must be admitted that there is one serious difficulty in the way of the acceptance of this great conclusion. The world is full of evil. How can the existence of evil be reconciled with this belief in the Supreme Power as utterly trustworthy ? This is the problem which most of all presses upon thoughtful minds in our day, and the difficulty has been terribly accentuated by the horrors which have accompanied the present awful worldwar.

Two ways of dealing with this problem have

been prominent in recent discussion. First, there are some who hold that the existence of evil proves that God is not, in the fullest sense, omnipotent. He is overcoming the evil, and will, we must believe, finally conquer it ; but, as things are now, the world is not altogether subject to Him. To this doctrine there is the objection that, if we suppose God's power limited in this way, we deny His supremacy, we admit an opposing power which, for all we can tell, may overcome Him and bring His work to nought. More fundamentally, we cease to regard Him as the Power which the universe manifests to us, we admit another and opposing power manifested in the universe and therefore we shake the foundation on which our faith is built.

A higher thought affords help here. May not the limitation of the Divine power be due, not to an opposing power standing in some sense on the same level of being, but to voluntary self-limitation ? The existence of finite beings, possessed of moral faculty, able to choose between good and evil, points to such self-limitation on the part of God. It would appear to be a condition of the very existence of a moral universe comprising a multitude of finite intelligences. This is the solution that has perhaps appealed most widely to thoughtful modern Christians. God desires children to love Him, not machines rendering a mechanical service. He has therefore created beings capable of good and also capable of evil, and to make this possible has limited, to some extent, the sphere of His own Divine power. But such limitation is not absolute. It is altogether relative to the accomplishment of His own supreme

C

purpose. That purpose is the final establishment of the Kingdom of Love, through the victory of Love over all the oppositions of evil wills. Evil is therefore essentially subordinate.

The second mode of dealing with the problem of evil enables us to gain a further view as to the nature of this subordination. It is admitted that, so far as we can see at present, the problem of evil is not fully soluble by our intelligence. May not this be a sign that our faith goes beyond our thought? We try to present to our minds the nature of God by means of ideas and language which belong to our human experience, but these ideas, and the terms which express them, are not adequate. The nature of God cannot be fully expressed in human language. As He is the Power manifested in the universe, while we are but elements in His universe, we must be inferior to Him in the scale of being, and therefore we may expect to find difficulties, insoluble to our thought, standing in the way of our perfect apprehension of His nature. But here religion may find comfort in the experience of science. Science finds herself constantly confronted with difficulties, but never for one moment does she lose hold of the principle of the constancy of Nature, and in that faith she conquers. So let it be with religion. She encounters problems more terrifying than those of science. For her also salvation must come through faith, that fundamental faith in the trustworthiness of the Supreme Power which is the very same as the faith in the constancy of Nature which guides Science to her victories.

It is worth our while to consider that there is a

point of view to which we can attain by help of modern philosophy, from which, it would seem, we can behold all these various elements of thought in larger perspective. We saw that man's faith in God begins with his inevitable tendency to project his own conscious nature into the world about him, and to find a spiritual origin for the things and events which affect his life. Is there any reasonable foundation for that tendency or is it based on illusion ? It is important to observe that modern philosophy has yielded a method of regarding the universe which discloses a remarkable significance in the impulse of the savage mind to find spirit everywhere.

What is spirit ? A spirit is a being who has experience. All things and events of which we are aware come to us as elements in our experience. To be a spirit is to be a being who is capable of grasping things and events within his experience. That is, a spirit is able to know, to feel, to think, to will. We may say that spirit is capacity in relation to experience. But it is more than capacity, it is also activity in relation to experience, because in will and in attention, which is necessary for knowledge, spirit is active. But how does the world exist at all ? There can be only one satisfactory answer to that question : the world exists as experience. All we know of the world, every sample we have of it, is experience. It can be nothing else. That is, all we know of the world exists only as contained within the capacity of some spirit. And not only so, but in every sample of the world, as it comes within our grasp, there is some degree of determination by the activity of spirit, because attention and will determine very largely the shape which our experience takes.

Now, surely we must believe that the world as it exists apart from our experience of it is the same sort of thing as it is in our experience. That rose, those trees, those hills, are the same whether I look at them or not. If that be so, it means that there is a universal experience in which the whole world of knowable things is included. And if so, there must be a capacity to grasp this universal experience. Or, in other words, there is a universal spirit. The world exists because God is. Thus we grasp the fact that God is Universal Personality : He is the Self, Subject, or Person, to whom the whole universal order of things is relative.

Having arrived at this conclusion, a further question arises. What is the relation of the finite human spirit to God ? To answer this we must consider the relation of the finite experience to the world as a whole. One thing is clear. This experience of mine is, somehow or other, a partial apprehension of that great universal experience— which I call the universe. Only by assuming that the universe is an experience in which I have a share can I be assured that the rose which I see and touch and smell is a real thing existing, with its colour, texture and perfume, just as I know them, in a world of similar character. My possession of conscious experience is my share in the life of God. " In Him we live and move and have our being."

God is the All-inclusive Life which comprehends all finite persons and their varying experiences. This must be so because every finite person has a share in His life. He must therefore be higher in the scale of being than any human person, for human personality does not possess this capacity to include other persons within its life. In Him, therefore, we must conclude, personality reaches a degree of unity higher than any form of unity known to our thought, a unity which can comprehend distinct persons within itself.

We may put it thus: There are degrees of reality, life is higher in the scale than matter, personality is higher than mere vitality, God is highest of all. We cannot ascend to the highest point of view and solve all problems.

This doctrine is quite opposed to pantheism. The latter identifies God and the universe: it regards the history of the universe as, in all its details, the history of the life of God. The doctrine here set forth thinks of God as above the universe, as well as working in the universe. His is the life which makes the whole possible, yet all that happens in that whole is not His work, just as a man's experience contains many things for which he is not responsible. Thus the problem of evil, however perplexing to us, need not destroy our faith in the supremacy of God.

(3) The final question that we set before ourselves in this paper is, Can man know God by actual experience? The testimony of devout souls in all ages affirms the possibility. The great literature which discloses the thoughts and strivings of those who have diligently sought after God reveals the fact that such have ever been convinced that it was possible to find Him, and that in numberless cases they had actually enjoyed that supreme

experience. The simplest illustration which can be given is the sense of presence which is attained in sincere prayer. The soul which shuts out the world and seeks God within is able to hold converse with the Unseen. The things of sense seem, for the time, to fall away, and the finite spirit meets the Infinite and feels Him to be the greatest of all realities. Is that illusion ? Surely not. If it be true that we share in the life of God, that in Him we live and move and have our being, then surely there is reason to think that we can become aware of the greater life enveloping our little life. Conscious of our own finiteness, we become aware of the Infinity of Being in which we dwell, and approaching that Being through the medium of spirit, and not through the medium of our limited abstract dealings with the material world, we feel His presence as the Personal Presence of One infinitely greater than we are, One Whose relation to us may be expressed by the great words : " The Eternal God is thy dwelling-place, and underneath are the everlasting arms."

NOTE.—The spiritual philosophy sketched above is easily justified against *Materialism*, which regards matter as the only true reality; for matter is known to us only through the medium of our consciousness. Also against *Naturalism*, which regards human life as a mere part of Nature ; because Nature is known through experience, and experience presupposes a conscious subject, or person. A doctrine of *Realism* which has recently appeared seems more dangerous. It holds that the world exists apart from spirit in the form of sensibles and universals. But how are these combined to form a whole ? In our experience, the combining agency is always that of a subject or person.

For recent discussions of the philosophical questions raised above, see H. Rashdall, *Philosophy and Religion*, and his article in *Personal Idealism* ; C. C. J. Webb, *Problems in the Relations of God and Man* ; and the writer's *God and Freedom in Human Experience*. On the controversy with Naturalism, see J. Ward, *Naturalism and Agnosticism*, and A. J. Balfour, *Foundations of Belief*, and *Theism and Humanism*. A. C. Fraser's *Philosophy of Theism* is very valuable.

III

THE MEANING OF THE INCARNATION

"And in Jesus Christ His only Son our Lord, who was conceived by the Holy Ghost."

IT is unnecessary to insist on the supreme attraction of the character of our Lord as portrayed in the Gospels. It is felt by all, and there are few, even among those who do not accept the teaching of the Apostles concerning His divine Person, but wish, and to some extent try, to become like Him. If that attempt is made with anything like constancy it may be held to mark a man as a Christian, though not as a Churchman. He is, so far as the past can ever be repeated, in the position of the Galilæan disciples before the Resurrection. But it may be doubted whether it is possible for any one to continue in such a position without development. It was not possible for those first disciples. Their love and admiration were connected with the thought of the Kingdom of God, and the relation of our Lord to it. His proclamation that the long-desired Kingdom was at hand had first drawn them to Him. In Him they saw, what had been looked for till then in vain, absolute fidelity to the pure ideal of that Kingdom. Here, in this positive form and not in the mere impossibility of catching Him in a fault, we perceive from the first the recognition of His perfect goodness. And from His lips, too, they heard an accent of authority different from any that had been heard before. "The time is fulfilled, and the kingdom of God is at hand : repent ye, and believe in the good tidings" (Mark i. 15) went beyond any message which the prophets had introduced with their "Thus saith the LORD." When the end of the ministry was approaching, and the Lord put the question, "Whom do men, whom do ye say that I am ? " St. Peter's answer brought to clear expression what was doubtless moving in the mind of others besides the Twelve. "Thou art the Christ," St. Peter said, and in that title at least one-half of what we mean by the Godhead of our Lord was implied. "The Christ"—i.e. "the Anointed of the LORD"— had indeed been the designation of all the kings of Judah from Saul onwards. In 2 Sam. vii. it is explained as including the relationship of a son to God as Father. That might have degenerated into a simple metaphor. But in the actual course of Jewish faith quite the contrary took place. The post-exilic Jewish Church, reading in the books of Isaiah and Daniel the same great vision as we read, of One to come who was to be named "Mighty God, Everlasting Father, Prince of Peace" (Isaiah ix. 6), whose dominion was to be "an everlasting dominion, which shall not pass away, and his kingdom that which shall not be destroyed" (Daniel vii. 14), deepened their conception of the Messiah, the Christ, in the same direction as we have deepened it in Christian thought. When our Lord was born, a world of

hopes were stirring Jewish minds of a Kingdom
of God which would not be of this world, and of
a Christ, the Son of God, the herald and prince of
that Kingdom, Who should be recognised as divine.

No doubt these hopes were various—not always
purely spiritual. No doubt the term " divine "
is more precise than the vague hopes of those
preparatory days. What the disciples found in
their Lord Jesus was a power, of a strangely
unexpected kind, which brought unity and precision into this variety and vagueness : " In
Jesus Christ all contradictions are reconciled."
We discern the process beginning in the early
chapters of the Acts. It is St. Paul who brings it
to full effect. He had not known Jesus of Nazareth
in " the days of His flesh," and though he felt
as all do the attraction of His character, that
character was displayed to him in the Lord's
death for the sake of men, and in the great act
of God which set the seal to His Christship, the
Resurrection : He was " born of the seed of
David according to the flesh, declared to be the
Son of God with power, according to the spirit
of holiness, by the resurrection of the dead "
(Romans i. 4). From this all the rest of St.
Paul's large creed sprang : " God was in Christ
reconciling the world unto himself : Him who
knew no sin he made to be sin on our behalf ;
that we might become the righteousness of God
in him " (2 Cor. v. 19, 21) ; Christ is " the image
of the invisible God, the firstborn of all creation ;
for in him were all things created . . . He is
before all things, and in him all things consist "
(Col. i. 15-17) ; and St. Paul associates the name

of Jesus Christ with the Father and the Spirit in a divine Trinity, "The grace of our Lord Jesus Christ, and the love of God, and the fellowship of the Holy Ghost, be with you all " (2 Cor. xiii. 14).

In all this St. Paul was but following out the most advanced Jewish doctrine of his time, as he himself claimed according to Acts xxiv. 14 *f.*; only, he believed the hope of his people to be realised in our Lord Jesus Christ. There is no infringement upon that doctrine of the " one God " on which the Jew so earnestly insisted. And we, too, must insist on that if we would think of the Incarnation as Holy Scripture directs us. " Jesus the believer's God " is far from scriptural language. Even such a compound term as " the God-man " somewhat jars upon an ear attuned to the New Testament ; at least it must not be allowed to suggest either that in Jesus Christ apart from the Father we worship God, or that His manhood is different in kind from the manhood of all men. The strong, one might almost say the daring, monotheism of St. Paul is remarkably illustrated by his vision of " the end " in 1 Cor. xv. 28 : " And when all things have been subjected unto him, then shall the Son also himself be subjected unto him that did subject all things unto him, that God may be all in all." It would be hazardous to pretend to fathom the profundity of this. But St. Paul does appear to be inspired with some great idea of a time or state in which all such terms as " Son," " Christ," " Trinity," must prove inadequate to picture the ultimate fulfilment of the rich unity of Godhead.

Here St. Paul shows the masculine intellect

with which he was endowed. But generally he dwells on the moral side of doctrine. To himself the revelation of Christ had come as an overpowering moral force. Shame, hope, love, trust, were wakened in him. He passed from moral impotence under the Law to a new life according to the Spirit of holiness. And this he knew to have been brought about by Christ's death and victory through death. This leads us first to notice the general truth—that the doctrine of .the Incarnation makes its essential appeal to our moral sense. It is indeed a doctrine of inexhaustible interest to the intellect. Yet it may be grasped with little or no intellectual exercise by those to whom such exercise on sacred subjects is uncongenial. On the other hand, all dispute about it which is empty of moral interest is certain to go wrong. If we try to treat it as a purely intellectual matter, questions soon take a form which renders them unanswerable; they pass from the region of "reality" into that of "appearance," like the questions, "Was there a beginning of time?" "Is there a limit to space?" This is in fact true of all "spiritual" ideas. Sooner or later we are compelled to shape them in terms of moral goodness, else discourse becomes barren; so, for instance, when we try to think out St. Paul's "spiritual body." To this consideration we shall return later.

But besides this, the form which the revelation of Christ took for St. Paul brings another point to our notice which will again and again come up in all thought about the Incarnation. The truth as he saw it was not as he would have expected to see it; the great fact was what we style paradoxical. His Jewish ancestors and teachers had been looking for the Christ. But it was a new thing to find the proof of Christship in a death of shame and apparent defeat. This is another point, yet it brings us quickly back to what we have just been considering. Christ's death was shameful as His ministry had been obscure. But reflection shows that we can conceive of no other way in which an equal moral grandeur could have been achieved. If "God was in Christ reconciling the world to himself"—and that is the essence of the Incarnation—anything commonly accounted fame or success would have been a vulgar shift; "sacrifice," the ideal of Christ's humility, stands alone among the activities possible to man as absolutely akin to the divine love.

In the prologue to the Gospel according to St. John the Incarnation is approached from another side. "In the beginning was the Word, and the Word was with God, and the Word was God . . . all things were made by him . . . in him was life." Here is an idea which had been in the mind of Greek philosophers; more lately, in the mind of some Jews also. God, Who in Himself would be beyond the reach of human comprehension, has made Himself manifest through His Word, by Whom creation has been wrought, and in Whom all created life has its being. "And the life was the light of men . . . There was the true light, even the light which lighteth every man, coming into the world." Here is a further thought. This Word is also to be recognised in man; in his intellect, but still more in the faculty with which man is endowed of communion with the divine; for here, too, the moral aspect chiefly interested even the philosophers of the Gentiles. And they, too, would partly understand the hope indicated in the last phrase, " coming into the world "; for they too had vague aspirations which are seen, when once the idea has been defined, to be summed up in the thought of Incarnation. Yet from the actual fact of Incarnation, of God coming in the real nature of man, to dwell as a man among other men, and that in lowliness and obscurity, these thinkers would have shrunk. Again, as with St. Paul so with St. John, the thing expected was realised in an unexpected manner. " And the Word became flesh and dwelt among us."

That is what St. John most insists upon. Unlike St. Paul, he is filled with the recollections of our Lord's life as very man among men on earth. That was why he wrote his Gospel. In an actual history, the wonder of which arises, sacramentally, out of its lowliness and simplicity, he finds the only way of really interpreting the vast idea of the Word Who was from the beginning with God and Who was and is God.

> And so the Word had breath, and wrought
> With human hands the creed of creeds
> In loveliness of perfect deeds,
> More strong than all poetic thought ;
>
> Which he may read that binds the sheaf,
> Or builds the house, or digs the grave,
> And those wild eyes that watch the wave
> In roarings round the coral reef ;

or, as the Evangelist himself puts it : " The Word dwelt among us, and we beheld his glory, glory as of the only begotten from the Father, full of grace and truth."

St. Paul, then, from the Jewish side carried on the first disciples' reverence for the great Master into the belief in Jesus as the Christ, the Son of God, associated with the Father in the unity of Godhead. St. John, with a wider approach, carried it on into the belief in Jesus as the Word of God Who is God. St. Paul's conception of the Incarnation might be summed up in the sentence, " God was in Christ reconciling the world to himself " ; St. John's in " The Word became flesh and dwelt among us." The passage from St. Paul is taken from an Epistle, 2 Corinthians, which needs no critical defence. Even if it be allowed that the date and authorship of the Fourth Gospel present complicated questions— that is a fairer way to put it than to speak of " difficulties "—still it must be insisted upon that the deeper modern criticism goes the more evident it becomes that behind all the apostolic writings there lies a popular and primitive tradition which enshrined a surprisingly high view of the Person of Christ. We can have little doubt that, first on the line of Jewish thought about the Christ, and soon after on the more universal line of thought about the Word, the primitive Church rose to belief in the Incarnation. St. Paul and St. John did not start that belief ; they guided it in more scrupulous reverence and reasonableness. Above all, they insist on its being realised practically and morally in our own daily life.

Few, however, who read this paper are likely to feel the critical difficulties acutely. It is not impossible that some may feel another kind of difficulty. Perhaps it might be described as the difficulty of common sense. What is meant will be seen if such persons will compare together two passages from which quotations have already been made, Romans i. 1-7 and Colossians i. 13-20. They may say, "The first of these passages I readily accept; the second demands an assent of quite another kind. In Romans I seem to read of a man uniquely inspired, to whose life continued after death—the like of which I would fain hope for other men—God vouchsafed unique testimony; in Colossians of One who is so absolutely divine that I cannot also recognise him as a man. I do not question the earliness, nor even the correctness of this belief. But it is so extraordinary, that I do hesitate to accept it whole-heartedly as my own." A fair, because a scriptural, answer would be this: The doctrine of the Incarnation does call for something more than our common sense. It demands our recognition of something wonderful in life. But it is in all life, not separately in the Person of our Lord, that this wonderful element is to be recognised. The Godhead of our Lord is never represented in the New Testament as separating Him from us. It is because He is God that He can overpass the limits which divide person from person in ordinary experience. In Him life and love are deepened; we live in Him and are joined together in Him. For himself, St. Paul expresses this effect of the Incarnation in Galatians ii. 20: "I have been crucified with Christ; yet I live; and yet no longer I, but Christ liveth in me." And though few would dare to say that they can as yet make this claim their own, it does describe the ideal to which each believer hopes he is progressing. Of the whole company of believers St. Paul continually asserts that they live " in Christ " : the phrase is characteristic of him, and the thought runs through all his teaching, his rebukes, and his encouragement. " Common sense " is apt to treat such sayings as forcible metaphors. But that recognition of a wonderful capacity in life, set free by the Incarnation, reverses the position. This union in Christ Who lifts men to God by virtue of His own Godhead is reality; the separations of our imperfect intercourse in the flesh are the shadows. If ever heart does reach another heart in fine thought or great deed it is because common life has been lifted up through Him—" That life which I now live in the flesh I live in faith, the faith which is in the Son of God, who loved me and gave himself up for me." Once more, as we noticed above and shall have to notice again, doctrine comes to effect in the spiritually moral region. Christ's love and sacrifice, our being crucified with Him; these are the conditions which, on the one hand, were made possible by the Incarnation, and, on the other hand, it is when these conditions become the main interest of life that the Incarnation is experienced as effectual.

In the Epistle to the Ephesians this idea of our living " in Christ " is worked out more distinctly. Here the ancient Jewish conception of the representative Christ—the Lord's Anointed Who represents or includes the whole nation (*cf. e.g.;* Psalm lxxxix. 51 ; Hebrews xi. 26)—is developed. " Christ " in this Epistle does of course mean the Lord Jesus. But it means more than " Jesus." It means Jesus exalted to the right hand of the Father, and now, in His Godhead enriched with manhood, gathering in, as part of Himself, all who follow and believe in Him. They are to grow with and in Him unto one " full-grown man, unto the measure of the stature of the fulness of Christ " (iv. 13). The thought appears very remarkably in i. 23, which should be translated ". . . the church, which is his body, the fulness of him who is being all in all fulfilled " ; see the Dean of Wells' *Exposition* of the Epistle, a small book in which this apostolic doctrine may be almost said to have been recovered for our generation. Not that it has ever been really lost. Tennyson's lines in *In Memoriam,* cvi, enshrine it :—

> Ring out, wild bells . . .
>
> Ring in the valiant man and free,
> The larger heart, the kindlier hand ;
> Ring out the darkness of the land,
> Ring in the Christ that is to be.

So, according to the more generous interpretation of the clause, does the Athanasian Creed : ". . . One Christ ; One ; not by conversion of the Godhead into flesh : but by taking of the manhood into God." And when we adopt from Ephesians the designation of the Church as " the body of Christ," we mean the same ; no mere metaphor, but a plain truth as real as it is wonderful. And by " real " we must understand " practical "

D

—that is, as we have already observed, spiritually moral.

The First Epistle of St. John is a treatise on the Church considered as the extension of the Incarnation. The opening verse gives the theological theme; the rest of the Epistle works it out in practical precepts about brotherly love. In the brethren we see the Incarnate Christ manifested. That is why Christian charity passes so far beyond common sense in this earliest manual of "Christian socialism": "We know that we have passed out of death into life, because we love the brethren" (iii. 14); "Hereby know we love, because he laid down his life for us: and we ought to lay down our lives for the brethren" (iii. 16); "Herein is love made perfect with us . . . because as he is, even so are we in this world" (iv. 17).

It should, however, be noticed that the term "Church" does not occur in this Epistle. The Church may be described as an extension of the Incarnation. But if the Incarnation does not extend also on other lines beside the line of the Church, at least it seems likely that, as the extension proceeds, we must expect to see the Church gathering strength by interaction with much that is as yet outside the boundary. No doubt St. John meant by "the brethren" those who had been baptised and were living in the community of Christ. In his day the division between these and "the whole world lying in the evil one" was unmistakable. But the light which came into the world with the Incarnate Word "lighteth every man" (John i. 9). It would dull the keen edge of St. John's precepts for ourselves if we still considered the brothers whom he bids us feed, clothe, love, and die for, as simply Churchmen. St. John insists on this love of the brethren being not " in word and with the tongue, but in deed and truth." In our modern way we should say that it must not be merely academic. Love has perhaps grown somewhat cold of late because we have become too academic. We try to plan a unity for the Church on the model of past centuries; but can any unity be really spiritual which does not transform the present enmity of nations ? We have explained the sacraments, and with sincere reverence guarded the approach to the altar ; and still our communion in the Body and Blood of Christ hardly affects the divisions between wealth and poverty, labour and capital. And meanwhile the boundaries are being blurred. Men are passing to a closer following of Christ who are not Churchmen, and some are striving with new boldness of self-sacrifice to realise the meaning of " we who are many, are one bread, one body," without caring, as things are, to " partake of the one bread " (1 Cor. x. 16 *f*.).

It is not easy to set forth a definite remedy for such a state of things. But there is perhaps no need to propose rash remedies. As to St. Paul, when the quiet of his imprisonment succeeded to faithful labour in the midst of " fightings without, fears within," the idea of the one Church descended and harmonised his " care of all the churches," so once again the idea of the one Church may be renewed, not by our anxious planning, but for us by God. Only, it is perhaps encouraging to

remember that the light of the Incarnation prepares
us for a manifold and unexpected development of
the Church, and that the designation of the Church
as " the body of Christ " is employed in Ephesians
less to imply visible boundary than living growth ;
it is in closest connexion with the living and
growing doctrine of the Incarnation.

For growth, too, belongs to the doctrine.
Christ exalted is still Christ incarnate, and the
discourses and prayer in St. John's Gospel, xiii–
xvii, promise that through the Holy Spirit the
incarnate Word will continuously manifest Himself in history, and thought, and in all that gradual
deepening and harmonising of life by which we
are being led onward out of blind enmities and
selfish vanities into the rich effective fellowship
of God's purpose for His creatures. That seems to
be at least part of the significance of " I am the
way, the truth, and the life." And, illustrated
by the prologue to this Gospel, that saying of the
Lord appears to reach even beyond the destiny
of man, to (what St. Paul has also just touched
upon in Romans viii. 18-25) the destiny of all
created life, of nature. Two realms of thought
and feeling have been widely opened in the last
half-century. One opening has been by the
advance of natural science. The other has been
thus described: " The religious perception of
our time, in its widest and most practical application, is the consciousness that our well-being,
both material and spiritual, individual and collective, temporal and eternal, lies in the growth
of brotherhood among all men—in their loving
harmony with one another " (Tolstoy, *What is*

Art?). Both have been suspected as hostile to the strict faith. Already we have gone far towards perceiving that the suspicion was groundless. The doctrine of the Incarnation, as we ponder upon it more thoughtfully, and apply it more practically, leads us to anticipate still broader and more fruitful reconciliations. Erasmus wrote that " the Spirit of Christ flows forth more widely than our interpretations allow." We might speak in like manner of the Body of Christ, meaning that the hope which Erasmus threw out vaguely is capable of being worked out with precision in actual affairs.

A possible objection to all this may occur. Some one may say : " You have taken some ideas which are very general just now, and you have fitted them into the doctrine of the Incarnation. But there is no logical necessity to do so. All that is valuable in these ideas may indeed depend upon the doctrine of the Word of God, but would remain equally available though the Word had never become flesh. The life of the Lord Jesus is in itself beautiful and grand. You have shown how it came to be connected with these other ideas. But I do not see why I should not believe in these ideas without connecting them in any special manner with that life."

This objection overlaps the objection which was considered earlier in this paper, and the answer must be a development of the answer given there. But first, it may be admitted that minds are differently constituted, and that to some faith seems to be more stimulated by ideas than by persons. The doctrine of the Word, taken by itself, is nearer to an idea than to the devotion to a person. There seems, which to some is an attraction, more of the infinite in it. And just as it appeared allowable to recognise a degree of Christian faith in one who tried to follow the example of the Lord Jesus without accepting the deeper mystery of His Person, so, too, it may be that he whose heart is anchored in the Word enjoys a part of the Christian faith, even though his intellect is not much engaged by historical recollection of Jesus of Nazareth. Yet this faith is but elementary in either case; its worth lies mainly in its promise of growth. And those will feel this most to be true who most feel the difficulty of bringing the two lines together—the definite concrete life of a particular man on earth and the ideal life of the eternal Word. For in this, as in all serious problems, the difficulty is the measure of the reality on which the problem turns. If that reality is absolute, the final solution always remains beyond our reach. Yet, on the other hand, our associated efforts towards solution unite us in the love of truth, throw light on other perplexities which beset our mortal condition, and assure us that the aspirations of manhood, though baffled, do run out into eternity. And indeed, when it is recognised that the term " eternal " is not antithetical to " on earth " the difficulty begins to vanish. Eternal life, according to the teaching of our Lord, especially as that teaching is interpreted in St. John, does not begin after death or in another world. Here and now we may be living eternal life. The new life on which we start and start again after each repentance is the

eternal life. What shows our Lord lifted so high
above all other men is that He needed not such
repentances and always lived the eternal life
without interruption. Then when this presence
of eternity in earthly surroundings is recognised,
that wonderful element of which we have already
spoken grows larger and larger in all we have to
do with, till it appears as the gleam of reality in
things ; it is always on, in, and around us, while
the shadows that partly obscure it pass and
change. But the very centre of all this wonderful
life is the wonder of the Person of Jesus Christ,
and—though we dare not say all—yet most of
those who have learned to delight in this rich
marvel of universal life do find an inexhaustible
joy in entering ever more deeply into the mystery
of Christ's Person. He must be there as a definite
Person, a person in the manner in which we ourselves know personality, else interest flags ; for
even those who most enjoy ideas do find mere
ideas unsatisfying if they are long cut off from
intercourse with persons, and it is hard to imagine
any other way of tracing out the thought of
Incarnation than by approaching it through the
human manifestation of the incarnate Person. He
must also not merely partake as we do in the
eternal and universal ; He must possess it as His
own. Else there is no problem of His Person at
all, and therefore no key to the thousand kindred
problems which certainly do face us day by day.
How the two become one in Jesus Christ we never
succeed in determining. But the search carries
us ever nearer to all that we mean by naming Him,
and few who have started upon the search would

hesitate to confess that to give it up would be for them the impoverishing of all they care about.

Yet an argument which reaches no conclusion is unsatisfactory. Is not the failure but another instance of what has been already noticed more than once in this paper, the mistake of trying to treat a spiritual and moral interest as an intellectual problem ? Not that the intellect has no part to play in the matter. To suppose that would be stupid ingratitude to the great thinkers who have, to the glory of God and the benefit of sincere souls, devoted their faculties to the noblest of all studies, Christian philosophy. But these great men have never treated the subject as an intellectual problem pure and simple. So far as they have achieved their aim they have also recognised the moral element. Nor, of course, is a man's failure to appreciate the doctrine of the Incarnation generally to be accounted for by something wrong in his own moral character. Such cases are probably rare. What is meant is this. Most of us will do better if we come to the question from the side of our affections, our duties, and all that complex spirituality within us which we sum up in such terms as " heart," or " love of God." And as this paper has nearly reached its allotted length, the readiest way to proceed will be to take one or two illustrative examples.

First, then, the actual life on earth, the particular character of our Lord Jesus Christ as really and truly a man, is proved by our experience to be all-necessary for us to remember and reverence. For therein we have the only revelation of God's character which is absolutely trustworthy. The

Old Testament witnesses to a progressive revelation of God which may easily mislead if it is not completed by the Gospel.   In fact, it has again and again misled good men and induced them to be cruel, to enforce religion by violence, and so on. Our several consciences may too readily be biased, as most of us know.   And besides that, the best part of our conscience, public or private, has been shaped, to a degree no one can exactly measure, by the general acceptance for generations past of the standard of Christ.   Yet even so, we are apt to fashion God in the image of our desires and prejudices.   For the strange thing about the revelation of God in Jesus Christ is that it goes so contrary to what our fancy would have.   An obscure career ; all done by love, nothing by omnipotence, and many seeming failures ; no gloom nor aloofness but much simplicity in happiness, as in the pleasure of quiet talk with chance comers ; no far-laid plans, but loving trust, and this trustfulness shown both to the Father in heaven and to men ; a very beautiful, austere, yet kind and, so to say, " natural " treatment of sin and sinners, hardly ever wholly imitated by even the best of men ; final victory through tragic defeat : in short, sacrifice, the ideal of Christ's humility, sheer love.

Again, this earthly life is what alone can rouse us to that romantic loyalty which is the beginning and the perfection of faith for many, and these often the noblest of the faithful, such as martyrs and missionaries.   And if no touch of this loyalty be in our hearts our faith is almost sure to become dull and wearisome, sometimes to ourselves, sometimes to others. Of which kind of faith it may too accurately be affirmed that " that which is becoming old and waxeth aged is nigh unto vanishing away."

And yet "romantic loyalty" will sound but a meagre phrase to those who are at home in the New Testament. They will rather feel that it is only by virtue of the power derived from the life of Christ that we are enabled to live at the level of the Word. Only in Christ can we grip hold on the Word. The act of God, put out in the life of Christ on our behalf, is our sole qualification for living as the Word requires of us. Christ's historical manifestation is the sacrificial and sacramental means by which we receive our adoption into the fellowship of the Word. Only through the Spirit, released by the saving work of Christ on the Cross, did the Apostles arrive, by spiritual experience, at the doctrine of the Word. Few can hope to arrive where they arrived except by travelling the same road.

And, on the other hand, if no interest is taken in the Saviour's pre-existence, in all that which is implied in the sublime language of the Creed: " God of God, Light of Light, very God of very God . . . Who for us men, and for our salvation, came down from heaven," then we fall to such a low level as when we style our Lord " the Founder of Christianity." It is a sad, cold title, and it leads to a sad cold estimate of our most holy faith. We think of it as having begun, a new and local thing, twenty centuries ago. And we cannot but feel the misgiving that this religion among the other religions will sooner or later go the way of all particular religions, passing and being succeeded by another. But happily there is no such word as "Christianity" in Holy Scripture. Holy Scripture is full of Christ, and Truth, and Love, and Life ; the eternal Person with His eternal attributes. There has never been a time or place where He was not. Nor has any religion, worthy of the name at all, been wholly without Him. Nor dares, nor desires, any one who believes in the eternal Word, and knows aught of the love of Christ, to claim that his own creed, rite, church, holds the whole of Christ, or is unaffected by shadows that are not Christ.

Yet creed and rite and church are also divine. Not only through the things that are seen, but through the very imperfections of life here, we lay hold of the perfect and unchanging. Therein is the sacramental energy of life, which emanates from the supreme sacrament of the Incarnation of our Lord and Saviour Jesus Christ.

That thought, indeed, of the Incarnation as the supreme sacrament, the interpretation of the whole sacramental principle, runs through all we have been considering in this paper. In the Catechism we say that by this word "sacrament" we mean "an outward and visible sign of an inward and spiritual grace given unto us, ordained by Christ himself, as a means whereby we receive the same, and a pledge to assure us thereof." There the reference is to the two ritual sacraments of Baptism and Holy Communion, which our Lord ordained. But these were fitted for His purpose because they were not to be arbitrary observances, but a particular application of that unity and interfusion of the visible and the eternal with which God has enobled the whole of His creation. The Church sacraments were ordained by Christ ; all nature was created sacramental by Him Who is the Word. So St. Paul says that " the invisible things of him since the creation of the world are clearly seen, being perceived through the things that are made, even his everlasting power and divinity " (Rom. i. 20) ; and St. John has the same principle in view when he says : " He that loveth not his brother whom he hath seen, cannot love God whom he hath not seen " (1 John iv. 20). Keble's hymn, "There is a book who runs may read," is a popular exposition of the idea. Keble meant more than that the beauties of nature stir our minds with thoughts of God. He meant that these forms of natural life really are parts in the life of God, just as St. John meant that in the brother we really do see God, and in our loving service to the brother we really do reach God. So, too, our Lord says in the parable, " The King shall answer and say unto them, Verily I say unto you, inasmuch as ye did it unto one of these my brethren, even these least, ye did it unto me " (Matt. xxv. 40).

" Even these least " is important. The sacramental principle is not concerned with pretty fancies, ingenious analogies, or the impression made on the mind by pomp and grandeur. It is an extension of the scientific fact, that all physical life is one, into the reasonable assurance of faith that all life is one, that the natural is also divine. Hence the very limitations, and sometimes even the repulsive aspects of visible life are sacramentally manifestations and means of approach to the eternal. And this becomes clearer still when we recognise that in the Incarnation of our Lord Jesus Christ the whole of this sacramental faculty of life is illuminated, consecrated, and assured. If the Incarnation is what we believe it to be, in it " the invisible things of God, even his everlasting power and divinity " are, in a measure which explains and includes all other partial manifestations, "perceived through the things that are made "—*i.e.* through all the antecedents, circumstances, and pregnant limitations of the life of Him whom we call our Lord, and Who lived as a man of a particular nation, at a particular time and place on earth. No mistaken reverence must induce us to widen the sphere in which He manifested Himself by cutting away such natural conditions as may appear to our private judgement unworthy of His greatness. To say, for instance, that He is " representative Man " must not involve denial that He is " a man." The mysterious and the essential cannot be dissociated from the individual in any person, least of all in Him who is most personal. Again, no quality in Him is more mysterious than His vast but ever simplifying intellect ; yet it would "overthrow the nature of a sacrament" to remove the mystery by supposing that He knew more than other men simply because He was God.

All such refinements infringe upon the doctrine which the Church received from the Apostles— viz. that the Incarnate Christ is very God and also very Man, not a mixture of the two. He is not, as the Arians once feigned—whose mistaken reverence we repudiate in the "Nicene" Creed —a "heavenly Being," by so much less than God as He is more than man. We hold fast to the complementary truths, both the Manhood and the Godhead, both the costly sympathy and the prerogative to save. And the seeming contradiction is resolved in the reasonable principle of the one, universal life divine, which in Him first, and then proceeding from Him, links continuously the visible and limited with the eternal and complete.

The term "sacrament" has here been used in the broad sense which it often bore in the early Church. Of late it has been more often confined to a special significance, and some who read these paragraphs may complain of the writer's perversity in diverting a current word (which is moreover distinguished by peculiarly sacred associations) to unfamiliar meanings. He can only answer that no lesser word seemed adequate to the purpose; that the doctrine of the Incarnation itself is continually educating us to recognise divinity and sanctity rather in inclusive power than in unique privilege; and that, if dissatisfaction is felt, he welcomes the opportunity of adding a reference to the fine essay on "Sacraments" in *Lux Mundi,* by Francis Paget, late Bishop of Oxford.

IV

JESUS CHRIST AND HISTORY

" Born of the Virgin Mary suffered under Pontius Pilate."

THE Christian religion is in an eminent sense an historical religion. It has its foundations in a revelation made to man, and a deliverance wrought for man, in a particular generation of mankind, through a life then lived upon earth, through events which then occurred and took their place among all the events of the time.

This connection of our Faith with history we will now consider. It is a characteristic strikingly recognised in the Church's Creed. In successive clauses of its second paragraph we have a number of facts regarding Jesus Christ recited ; two of them—His Crucifixion when Pontius Pilate was governor of Judæa, and His burial—purely natural ones ; others—His Birth from a Virgin, His Resurrection and Ascension—having both a supernatural and a natural side, being such as are not comprehensible to the extent that facts falling within general human experience are, and yet are said to have happened at a definite moment of time, and became known through ordinary human channels.

Both these kinds of facts mentioned in the Creed derive their significance from the conviction

that is expressed about Him Whom they concern
—that He is the Christ, the Son of God. The fact
itself, for instance, that Jesus of Nazareth was
crucified, could only be regarded, if He was but
a very holy man and a great moral and spiritual
teacher, as one of the most appalling crimes recorded in human history, and the contemplation
of it would sadden and depress us. But interpreted in the light of what the Church believes
about Him, it becomes the greatest proof of the
love of God, the ground of man's hope of salvation,
and therefore fitly holds a place in the Creed of
Christendom, which is to the Church a song of
triumph.

We cannot, then, rightly view particular events,
concerning Jesus Christ apart from our whole
conception of Him, and this must be formed from
all that we can gather as to what He showed Himself to be. Even in the days of the Public Ministry
of Jesus and in the years that immediately followed
His Crucifixion faith in Him was a complex thing.
It did not arise solely from witnessing His miracles,
or from those " infallible proofs " that He had
risen from the dead of which the author of the
Acts speaks ; but, in addition to these, from the
whole effect of His personality upon minds morally
and spiritually in a condition to feel it, apart from
which neither miracles which He performed, nor
His own resurrection, ever sufficed, or could suffice,
to create faith.

It is, then, to the total impression, so to speak,
which He made that we have in the first instance
to turn, and we know what this was primarily from
the writings of the New Testament. Questions

as to the authorship and date of most of these
writings have been, and some of them still are,
much debated ; but with a view to the use now
to be made of them, it is necessary only to assume
conclusions on these points which have been very
widely accepted both by men who, while adhering
to the faith of the Church, have striven to weigh
evidence impartially, and also by many other
scholars occupying a more detached position.

For our present purpose we may divide the
writings of the New Testament into two classes—
namely, the four Gospels, which directly treat of
the subject of the Person and Work of Jesus Christ,
and all the remainder. The first of the latter in
order of position gives some account of the beginnings and early spread of the society of those who
believed in Him ; the subject of the last is His
present heavenly reign and the future complete
triumph of His Kingdom. All the others are in
the form of letters, most of them being addressed
to particular communities of Christians, and
dealing with questions of doctrine and practice
which had in the several localities caused trouble
or perplexity ; a few of them intended even
originally for the believers, not in one place, but
in different places, and approximating in character
to homilies.

It will be safe to say that, with the exception,
at most, of two or three of the minor Epistles, the
writings of the New Testament had all been composed by the end of the first or the beginning of
the second century—i.e. within seventy or eighty
years after the Crucifixion, and some of them as
early as twenty-five years after that event.

E

It will be well, I think, that before we turn to the accounts given of Jesus Christ in the Gospels we should fix our thoughts for a few moments on the other half of the New Testament. To do so will prepare us for rightly appreciating the meaning of the Gospel-story. The existence and faith of the Church of Christ have ever been the strongest testimony to Jesus Christ. And here in these writings, though they do not contain many references to incidents in His life on earth, or recite many of His sayings, we have the testimony to Him of the Church of the first days. We have an irrefragable demonstration of the marvellous effect produced by the Ministry and Death and Resurrection of Jesus. We are taken into the midst of that new and great movement which sprang from Him, and was inspired by the new hope which He imparted, and was ever drawing fresh strength from faith in Him. In the life which we can still feel throbbing in these documents, which we hold in our hands, we have evidence not to be gainsaid of the power of Jesus Christ over men's hearts.

It would be impossible within the limits of a short paper to indicate in the barest manner the contribution made in this respect severally by each of these writings. Let me single out for brief consideration certain of St. Paul's Epistles. There are four of these of which the authenticity was admitted by the school of critics which has gone furthest in combating traditional views of the New Testament and of early Christian history, and which is so almost universally now, on account of the unmistakable signs of genuineness in their tone and character. These Epistles are the two

to the Corinthians, that to the Galatians, and that
to the Romans. All these had been written before
A.D. 57 at the latest. There are other of the
Epistles attributed to him which from internal
marks appear unquestionably to be his. I would
name especially the Epistle to the Philippians,
written four or five years after the four which
have just been mentioned, when he was a prisoner
at Rome.

These Epistles amply enable us to determine
what St. Paul's own faith was, and what that
Gospel was which he felt himself called to preach
as widely as he could, and the basis on which they
rested. His whole view of God's purposes and of
the way of salvation for man had been transformed
through arriving at the conviction that Jesus, Who
had suffered upon the Cross, was the Christ, and
that by this path He had entered into His glory.
By continual reflection upon these facts fresh
points in regard to their significance doubtless
presented themselves to His mind. This had been
the case before, and in all probability continued
to be so after, he wrote the Epistles that I have
named. But there is clear evidence in those
Epistles themselves that the foundation of his
belief and teaching, and in the most important
respects their substance also, had remained the
same throughout. In the Epistle to the Galatians
and in the First Epistle to the Corinthians he
appeals with the utmost confidence to what he
had taught those addressed when he first came
amongst them, as being identical with what
he taught still. In the former he pronounces
anathema on those who should preach any other

Gospel (Gal. i. 8, 9). In the latter, at the beginning of his great argument on the Resurrection, he refers to what he had delivered to them concerning appearances of the Risen Christ. Not only so, but he states also that what he " delivered " he had himself " received " (1 Cor. xv. 1 *ff.*). It is noteworthy that, although the revelation to himself on the road to Damascus must have had peculiar weight with him, he gives the first place to that which he had " received "—namely, the testimony of the older apostles. For the time that he " received " it we must go back well-nigh to the beginning of the preaching of the Christian faith. His conversion took place not improbably within two or three years, and certainly not more than six years, after the Crucifixion. It is most likely that, while the appearance of Jesus Christ to himself was decisive in bringing about the great change in all his views, a preparation for it had already been going on for some time. He was bidden no longer to " kick against the goads " (Acts xxvi. 16). He had been brought into contact in a hostile manner with eminent disciples of Jesus in Jerusalem, and that which they said had, we may well suppose, made a deep impression upon him, energetically as he had striven in his own mind to resist it. At all events, immediately after his conversion he must have been instructed in the statements which the eye-witnesses were accustomed to make. St. Paul's testimony, then, to the Gospel history, so far as it is given, affords a strong link with that of the first days.

Moreover, the connection is of a broader kind than at first sight appears. It is true that the momentousness of two outstanding facts—the Crucifixion and the Resurrection of the Son of God—seems for St. Paul's mind to have overshadowed all else in that history. Yet it should be observed that the reality of the death of Jesus, in which he plainly believed, involved his true humanity ; and, further, in what has been often said as to his indifference to the earthly life of Jesus there is plainly, to say the least, a great deal of exaggeration. It is not conceivable that one who held up the example of Jesus Christ in that " though He was rich, yet for your sakes He became poor " (2 Cor. viii. 9), and who marked the successive steps in His humiliation of Himself, noting first that " He took the form of a servant, being made in the likeness of men " (Phil. ii. 7, 8), should not have dwelt at times in his own thoughts and in his preaching on particular incidents or features of His life on earth, which illustrated the general conception ; or that he should not have sought to learn, and have communicated to others, sayings of the Lord, with the spirit of Whose ethical teaching, as it has been preserved for us in the Gospels, his own is in such striking accord.

But great as is the value of this comparatively indirect evidence of the influence of Jesus, we turn with even deeper interest to the professed records of His life, and ask whether we may regard them as trustworthy. It was primarily the duty committed to that chosen body of twelve disciples, who were specially close attendants upon Jesus during His Ministry on earth, to relate His deeds and His words, as well as to bear witness to His appearances to them after He had risen from the dead.

It is clear that for many years they gave this information and testimony orally, and it was not (it would seem) till some of the chief among them had passed away by a martyr's death, or otherwise, that the need began to be urgently felt in the Church for permanent records of what they had delivered. The earliest of these records which has come down to us, as few doubt who have studied the subject, is our Gospel according to St. Mark. We may with great probability assign its composition to A.D. 65, or some year not much later than this—*i.e.* to a time not much after the martyrdom, in the Neronian persecution at Rome, of St. Peter, whose follower and helper in the work of evangelisation St. Mark was. According to a very early statement quoted by the Church historian, Eusebius, Mark made it his aim to give a faithful account of what Peter had been accustomed to deliver in his preaching. But while we may believe St. Peter to have been his principal source of information, he must have known, and would naturally not have refrained from making use of, what other original disciples of the Lord had related. The great value for us, then, of this Gospel consists in the fact that, as there is good reason to think, it follows the general outline, and embodies the substance, of the teaching which some of the chief personal followers of Jesus during His Public Ministry were accustomed to give concerning His life and death, in response to the demand which, as they went about on their missionary work, was made of them for information about Him Whom they declared to be the Christ and to have risen from the dead.

The Gospels according to St. Matthew and St. Luke were probably written some few years after St. Mark, of which each appears to make use. But they also, besides much that is of great interest which is peculiar to each, contain matter derived from some common source, which was mainly, it would seem, a collection of the sayings and discourses of Jesus. The same authority from whom we learn St. Mark's dependence upon St. Peter tells us that the Apostle Matthew drew up an account of the Lord's teaching in the Hebrew language. From it that common matter to which I have referred in our First and Third Gospels is probably derived. We may well suppose that it may be somewhat more fully reproduced in our Greek Gospel according to St. Matthew than elsewhere, and that for this reason his name has been specially connected with that Gospel.

Both this document, which specially recorded our Lord's teaching, and our St. Mark, or a briefer form of that work, may be among the writings referred to by St. Luke at the beginning of his Gospel; and he probably had others in mind also, since he says that many had undertaken to draw up such accounts. In many respects they must have resembled each other, since they were all based upon the testimony of those who " from the beginning were eye-witnesses and ministers of the word." Some would be more, some less, full; but there is good reason to feel confident that the substance of them all is contained in our first three (so-called Synoptic) Gospels.

The composition of our Fourth Gospel must be placed near the end of that period of seventy or eighty years after the Crucifixion, within which, as I said above, if not quite all the writings of the New Testament, at least all the chief and most of the lesser of them were produced. This Gospel is the fruit of deep meditation upon the Person and Work of Christ, and in it the evangelist strives to represent to his readers the inner mind of Christ, and the full purport of His claims upon the faith of men. The questions of its authorship, and of the relation between its account of the life and teaching of Jesus Christ and that in the first three Gospels, are difficult, and a solution of them which commands wide assent has not yet been attained. But there is, to say the least, far deeper inner agreement between the view given us in this Gospel of the Person and Mission of Jesus Christ and that in the other three than is apparent at first sight, or than many critics have been, or even now are, willing to allow.

So far as to the sources of the Gospel history : one or two points only in that history, broadly viewed, can be touched on here.

Our Lord's own course of conduct in His Ministry among men, the hopes He raised, the questions asked about Him, the perplexities He caused, were all more or less closely connected with the expectation among the Jews of His time, implanted in their minds through their previous history and the teaching of the Old Testament prophets, and stimulated afresh by the Apocalyptic literature of later generations, that one should be sent to them from God—His Messiah—(or Christ)—Who should deliver Israel from sin and bondage, and that the Kingdom of God should be established upon earth. Jesus plainly implied that He had come to fulfil this Hope ; and yet, in the very act of holding out the promise that He would do so, He stripped it of its national limitations, and set before the minds of all who had spiritual discernment an entirely new conception of what is truly great upon earth. In order to work out redemption for men He Himself trod the path of self-abnegation and suffering. At the same time He exalted immeasurably the idea of the character and completeness of that redemption which He would accomplish. And He asserted that He had perfect knowledge of the Father's Will through a communion with Him which was absolutely unique. In spite of the lowliness of His life and " sweet reasonableness " of His general demeanour, He made claims for Himself which were tremendous. And yet there are none of the ordinary signs of fanaticism in His manner of making them. Indeed, we have a guarantee of the truth of what He declared, or led men to believe, about Himself in the marvellous insight which He showed into human character, and that thoroughness in the moral life and faultless sincerity in conduct and thought and motive, which He demanded. Such knowledge of others would be impossible without the fullest self-knowledge ; and such a standard could not be set before others by one whose own motives were not perfectly pure.

A few words must be said with regard to the miraculous element in the Gospel-history. There are, first of all, the wonderful works which Jesus is recorded to have performed. We cannot here inquire whether, as was maintained by Christian

Fathers and as has been held by many thoughtful theologians in modern times, the miracles of our Lord were (so to speak) a natural outflow from His Incarnate life. Nor can we examine indications in the Gospels of His own consciousness in respect to the power by which He worked them. We must be content to mark the place they occupied in His Ministry. Further, we can view them only collectively, but for our present object this will be most useful, while difficulties that may be felt about particular works thus become relatively of less importance.

If we consider the miracles of Jesus from the point of view of the Messianic expectation which prevailed, we cannot fail to see that they had a most intimate connection with the proclamation through His preaching of the Coming of the Kingdom of God. They were a revelation of God's redeeming purpose ; they compelled men to ask whether the time when there should be no more sorrow had not come, and whether this was not the promised Deliverer. In so doing they plainly served an important end in relation to His Mission. And while in themselves they afforded relief only for a time to a limited number of sufferers in that generation, they were a foretaste and pledge of that victory which should ultimately be won over pain and death.

Of a different order from the miracles which Jesus Himself performed are those of His birth from a Virgin and His resurrection. The evidence for the latter, which has been in part incidentally referred to above, will be more fully considered in another paper of this series. One or two remarks must be made on the evidence for the former.

The absence of any express mention of, or unquestionable allusion to, the Virgin birth elsewhere in the New Testament than in the opening narratives of St. Matthew and St. Luke has been a ground for questioning its truth. But there are considerations which go some way at least towards supplying a satisfactory explanation of this comparative silence. There was an outline of facts, which it was customary to relate in the early preaching of the Gospel. It began from "the baptism which John preached " and passed from this to the public ministry of Jesus (Acts i. 22 ; x. 37 ff. ; xiii. 23 ff.). We can see more than one reason for this point of departure having been chosen. The period covered fell within the personal knowledge of the twelve. In appealing also to Jews it was a most impressive introduction to the Gospel-history, that the work of the Baptist should be placed in the forefront as ushering in that of Jesus. It was natural also that for some time reserve should be practised on the subject of the miraculous conception. It was a mystery too sacred, and too capable of misrepresentation, to be at once publicly proclaimed. It was well that even converts should be instructed first in other parts of the Faith, and so prepared to place this article in due course in its right position.

The limits of St. Mark's Gospel were determined by those which had been usually observed in the oral teaching of the Gospel. Even in the Fourth Gospel there may be a trace of the influence of the old habit in oral narration, in the fact that a reference to the testimony of the Baptist to Jesus is woven into the Prologue, and that the first scenes described are connected with him. The most noteworthy point, however, to be observed in regard to the beginning of this Gospel, is that while the subject of the Eternal Being and Life of the Son of God, and the fact that He truly became Man, and lived as a man among men, are here dwelt upon, nothing is said as to the manner in which He took it. But there is no reason to think that the evangelist was therefore indifferent to what is related concerning the Birth of Jesus in our First and Third Gospels, with whose narratives he was in all probability acquainted. His mode of treatment in the present instance agrees with the characteristics of this Gospel generally, in which attention is directed rather to the great spiritual truths lying behind facts of history than to those facts themselves.

The differences between St. Matthew and St. Luke in their opening chapters are familiar to all readers of the Bible. It has often been pointed out that the former appears more especially to give the experiences of Joseph, and the latter of the Blessed Virgin. The sources from which the two Evangelists drew their information were plainly independent. It may well be urged that for this reason the two accounts confirm each other in regard to the main point in which they coincide, the miraculous manner of the Saviour's birth.

It is pre-eminently true of this article of the Christian Creed that our estimate of the evidence for it will be affected by what, quite apart from it, we believe as to the Person of Jesus Christ. If on broader grounds we are convinced of His true Divinity, there will seem to be a fitness in the mode of His incarnation having been supernatural, even though He truly united human nature to Himself, and placed Himself completely under human conditions in His life on earth.

The consideration applied in this instance leads on to a final observation with regard to belief in the miraculous element in the Gospel-history generally, or any portion of it. Those laws of Nature, as we are wont to call them, which have been formulated through the careful study of Nature, should be sacred in our eyes, for they represent the usual method of God's working. But it can never be said that they must cover all cases which may have arisen, or which may hereafter arise. The reasoning by which they have been arrived at, based as it is on a range of experience which is inevitably limited, cannot prove such necessary universality. The strength of the testimony, whatever it may be, for any alleged exceptions has therefore to be taken into account. But there are still considerations of another kind which may justly have weight with us—namely, those as to the ends which any particular miracle may appear to have served in the purposes of God ; and in judging of these the mind cannot but be influenced by its whole attitude with regard to things spiritual. Indeed, for the genuine Theist the question of the credibility of miracles, to whatever conclusion he is led, will be essentially a religious one : that is to say, he will interpret the evidence in the light of all that he can learn concerning the Divine Government of the world, through a right understanding of Nature and of History, and of what appears to have been required for carrying out the Divine plan for man's Redemption.

This short paper has been concerned with facts of history which happened long ago, and the sources of our knowledge of them. But let us not leave this subject without calling to mind how the present is connected with that distant past through that marvellous influence of Jesus which has extended through the centuries since, and reaches even unto us. This has to be taken into account if we would attempt to measure, however inadequately, the place of Jesus Christ in history. Far as even His professed followers in general have been, and are, from conforming themselves to His teaching, human thought and institutions have been profoundly affected by it, and human ideals of what is truly good and noble have been largely moulded upon it, wherever He has become known. Above all, to innumerable multitudes in every generation He has been, as He still is, an object of personal loyalty and devotion in a manner that is absolutely unique. Love in other cases is confined to those whom we have known in the flesh. We admire the great ones of former ages ; we feel an interest in anything that we can learn about our own ancestors ; we can say about one and another, of whom we have read or heard, that we are sure we should have liked or loved them *if* we had lived with them. That is all. But Jesus Christ is still loved and trusted and adored as a living Friend and Saviour and King.

JESUS CHRIST AND SIN

" Was crucified, dead, and buried, He descended into hell."

BEFORE we come to the interpretation of this article of the Creed, it is worth while to call attention again to what is set forth in the paper immediately preceding this one, the fact of the historical character of Christianity. The Church, as a teaching body, has always put the facts about Christ first, and based her theology upon them. She knows nothing of a theology or mysticism which is independent of definite, historical, concrete facts. The mention of Pontius Pilate was not due to a desire to pillory him as an exceptionally great criminal (he was not so regarded), but was intended to emphasise the reality of the Lord's suffering and death.

The words " suffered," " dead," are not found in the oldest form of the Creed. Their introduction emphasised the fact of the reality of what took place on the Cross. Christ, though He was the Son of God, submitted Himself to actual suffering and to what St. Paul calls " the last enemy "—death. The word " buried " deserves special notice, as we should hardly have expected its inclusion. What is its special importance that it should gain a place in a short Creed ?

Once more, the desire to insist on the historic reality of everything connected with the Passion is seen at work, as against those who taught that there was no real body of the Lord, and therefore no real death or burial, or that the Son of God left a merely human Jesus to die on the Cross, and Himself returned to the heaven whence He had descended upon the man Jesus at the moment of His baptism. The Creed will have none of such speculations. It is Jesus Christ the only Son of God Who died and was buried. But further, the word " buried " looks forward to the next article on the Resurrection precisely as it does in 1 Corinthians xv. 4, where St. Paul says that his " Gospel " contains the facts that Christ was buried, and rose again the third day. For St. Paul and for the Creed it is the Person Who was buried Who rose again. It is no mere continued existence after death, no return as of a ghost from another world. We do not speak of the burial of the soul, or the resurrection of the soul, but of the whole person who has been laid in the grave. It is evident that both St. Paul and the Creed hold and teach the belief in the empty tomb, that the Person laid there on Good Friday was not to be found there on Easter Day, and the word " buried " removes all possible doubt of their meaning.

Finally, the clause " He descended into hell " we find first in the Creed as it was recited in a little town in North Italy—Aquileia—in the fourth century A.D. But what it teaches is the teaching of quite early Christian writers, and of the First Epistle of St. Peter, who speaks of Christ as, after

His Crucifixion, preaching to the spirits in prison.
Moreover, it has the sanction of our Lord's word
to the penitent thief, " To-day shalt thou be with
Me in Paradise "—for Paradise is not Heaven,
just as Hell in the Creed is not Gehenna, the place
of torment, but the abode of departed souls, which
is what the Greek word Hades means. Of the
importance of this clause something will be said
later ; here let it suffice to point out that once
again the Creed assures us that the Lord after His
death went where man must go, and experienced
in His human soul, which by death had been
separated from His body, what man must experience.

We have seen that this article of the Creed not
only puts before us the Lord's Passion as something which we must, each individually, believe
in, but insists on the historical reality of the
Passion and of all that the Passion involved.
Now we must go a step further and ask : " Why
has the death of Christ a place in the Creed at
all ? " Why is it important to believe that He
was crucified and died ? For it is exceedingly
interesting to observe that in the Creed no single
event in our Lord's life, between His birth and
His death, finds a place. There is not a word
about His teaching or His miracles, and yet we
know very well that both teaching and miracles
were highly prized by Christians. Why then,
after confessing our belief in His birth, are we not
told to express our belief in any of His words and
works, but only in His death ?

Before we can answer this question satis-
factorily we must go back to the very beginnings
F

of the work of the Christian Church. We must fix in our minds, and turn over and over again in our minds, the great thought which the first apostles and disciples could never forget: Jesus had died—*and He was the Messiah*, that is, the Anointed One, in Greek the Christ. Remember what that meant. He to whom the Old Testament, the Bible of those Christians, pointed forward, had come. And instead of reigning in triumph, instead of openly and undeniably bringing into existence a glorious new state of things, He had been crucified and had died. True, He had risen again, but that did not in itself explain the death; neither death nor resurrection was expected of the Messiah. Why had He died at all? There must be some great meaning in that fact. Moreover, the death of Jesus was, as St. Paul was to call it, a stumbling-block, an offence, to those who stood outside the Christian community. Jews, from the first, taunted the disciples with the death of Jesus; He had been crucified—how could He possibly be the Messiah? And Gentiles were soon to mock at the folly of the idea that One who had been put to death as a criminal could be Saviour, Redeemer, Son of God. Clearly, the death of Jesus was a fact of the first importance; Jews and Gentiles laid stress on it in their attacks upon the Church, in order to discredit Jesus; on the other hand, if Jesus was what the Church believed, why had He died, and died in this way?

The New Testament is full of what we may call the Christian case on this matter. But before we say anything more, one very obvious but very remarkable fact must be noticed. In the New Testament the death of Christ, the Cross of Christ, is not at all spoken of as though it were an inconvenient fact which had to be defended or almost explained away, as though it were the weak point in the Gospel which the Christian missionaries began to preach in the world. Above all, it is not something to be hidden away, but something to be proclaimed and gloried in. In other words, the Church did not for a moment allow that Jews and Gentiles possessed a strong argument against Christianity in the fact that Jesus had been crucified, for one does not put into the forefront of one's teaching something which is felt to favour one's opponents. The deepest and most lasting note in the great chord of the Cross, as it echoes through the New Testament, is the note of triumph. Our inquiries must start from an acknowledgment of that fact.

Let us return to the thought—the Church from the very first looked on Jesus as the Messiah. What was it expected that the Messiah would be ? Among other things, and not the least important, He was to be the Deliverer, the Saviour. But from what would He save and deliver His people ? Not only from external tyranny or oppression, but also from their own sins and the results of those sins. The Old Testament as a whole is a record of the fact that though Israel was the chosen people, Israel was constantly out of touch with God because of Israel's sins. The prophets do not tire of warning the people that their high privilege of being God's people will avail them nothing if they will not put away their sins and turn to God in repentance and amendment. Accordingly, when the Messiah came He would show Himself the righteous ruler, executing justice and righteousness in the land, while Israel's sins (for it is the nation, rather than individuals, which appears as the sinner in the sight of God) will have been forgiven.

The two ideas of the coming of Messiah, of the Kingdom of God, of the Righteous Ruler on the one hand, and of the forgiveness of sins on the other, were inseparable, and could not but be so in a nation which alone of the great nations of antiquity took the idea of sin seriously, in representing the moral shortcomings and positive wickedness of man as an offence against a holy God and inevitably condemned by Him. Now, for the Christian Church Jesus was the Messiah. How then stood this matter of forgiveness and salvation? How was it affected by the fact that He, " the one who should come " (Matt. xi. 3), had come? What had He done in connection with it?

It was at this point that the fact of the Lord's death came into immediate prominence, its meaning lit up with the light which shone upon it from this quarter and that. In the first place, there were the Old Testament sacrifices; these were bound up with the thought of the forgiveness of sins. The sacrifices were not magical acts; they had no virtue of their own to ensure the forgiveness of sins; the gracious God alone could forgive sins. But that did not mean that the forgiveness of sins could not be brought into connection with, and work through, particular institutions or persons. So the sacrifices represented a connection between the forgiveness of sins and the laying down of life and the offering of that life to God. Once more—the greatest prophecy in the Old Testament is that contained in the last twenty-six chapters of the book of the prophet Isaiah. In the 53rd chapter of that book there was, to be read of all, the wonderful passage declaring that the violent death suffered by the mysterious Servant of Jehovah was endured by him, not because of his own sins but because of the sins of others—those others who should find themselves forgiven and profited by his bearing of their sins, sins laid on him by Jehovah. And besides all this, there was the fact that the Lord Himself had treated His death as a matter of the utmost importance, had described it as necessary, and as a ransom given for many, and had declared that in His blood shed for many there was a new covenant ; and of the new covenant, when it shall have been made between God and Israel, one of the characteristics, according to Jeremiah (xxxi. 34), is that Jehovah will forgive their iniquity and remember their sins no more.

In such considerations as these lay the Christian defence against Jews who thought to show that the followers of Jesus stood condemned by the fact of the Crucifixion of Jesus. But herein, too, lay the secret of that Christian triumph and exultation in the Cross which felt no shame, whether before Jew or Gentile, in what St. Paul calls (1 Cor. i. 23) the proclamation of a crucified Messiah. Almost all the New Testament writers put the Cross into a position of the greatest prominence. They do not all regard it from exactly the same angle, they do not all say the same things about it. Why should they ? If Jesus was the Messiah, then Messiah's death was too great a thing for any one man, even a St. Paul or a St. John, to grasp its full significance. The Holy Spirit did not lead the apostles into all truth by leading them to see and to express the same thing in the same way, but by enlightening their understandings so that each according to his ability might utter some part of the truth as it was in Jesus, and in Jesus crucified. So we find St. Peter teaching in his sermon on the Day of Pentecost that though the Jews had wickedly killed Jesus, yet the death of Jesus had its place in " the counsel and foreknowledge of God " (Acts ii. 23, and cf. iv. 28) ; Philip the deacon starts from the comparison of the Servant of Jehovah to the lamb taken to the slaughter, in Isaiah liii., to preach Jesus to the Ethiopian eunuch perplexed about the passage ; St. Paul tells the Ephesian elders that the Church of God which they superintend was purchased with the blood of God. Passing to the Epistles, there is an extraordinary wealth of allusions : for St. Peter, Christ is the One Who took away men's sins by bearing them " in His own body on the tree " (1 Peter ii. 24) ; for St. John, the proof of the love of God is the fact that He " sent His Son to be the propitiation for our sins " (1 John iv. 10), and the effect of the blood of Jesus is that Christians are cleansed from all sin (1 John i. 7) ; the writer of the Epistle to the Hebrews sees Christ as the true priest and true sacrifice ; the sacrifice of Himself once for all upon the Cross being the one real sacrifice of which the

Levitical sacrifices were but types, and to which
they pointed forward ; as for St. Paul, his letters
must be read closely and frequently if one is to
gather anything like a full impression of all that
he sees in the death of Christ. He tells the
Corinthians (1 Cor. ii. 2) that when he came to
them he was resolved not to know anything
among them "save Jesus Christ and Him crucified,"
and his message to us is the same as his message
to the Corinthian Church. What did not the
Lord's death mean to him ? In it he saw the
propitiation of God, the satisfaction of God's
justice, God's wrath against sinners brought to an
end, the reconciliation of God and man ; yet all
this not as though Christ had intervened as a third
between God and man, but " God was in Christ
reconciling the world unto Himself, not imputing
their trespasses unto them " (2 Cor. v. 19). And
the joint love of the Father and the Son for man
in the Cross of Christ is most strikingly presented
when, after saying how wonderful a thing it is
that Christ has died not for the righteous but for
sinners, the Apostle continues : " But God com-
mendeth His love towards us, in that, while we
were yet sinners, Christ died for us " (Rom. v. 8).
Or think again of the great passage in Colossians
(i. 19, 20) : " It pleased the Father that in Him
should all fulness dwell ; and, having made
peace through the blood of His cross, by Him to
reconcile all things unto Himself." Nothing is
more necessary than to take St. Paul's teaching as
a whole, and that whole includes at least these
elements : sin necessarily calls down the anger of
a holy God and deserves punishment ; God's wish

was not to destroy sinners but to forgive and save
them, while revealing Himself as a God Who
cannot treat sin as though it were not of all evils
the worst ; God gives His Son to be incarnate, to
be obedient even unto the death of the Cross ; by
His life, and above all by His death, Christ does
for man and as man what man could not have
done for himself, for sinful man could never have
made atonement and reparation to God for his sins,
but this is what the sinless Christ effects by His
perfect obedience, and by His willing submission
to death, in which is seen God's penalty upon sin.
Finally (and here St. Paul's thought reaches its
climax, to which it is not easy for us to ascend,
but which does not entirely escape our understanding), Christ on the Cross, though He was
always the beloved Son, though any thought of
the wrath of God directed against Him as a Person
could not be entertained for a single moment,
experienced, because He was truly man, one with
sinful humanity though Himself sinless, the meaning of God's wrath against sin, and of the penalty
which sin must incur. Into that experience Christ
entered, and that is what St. Paul means when he
speaks of Christ as " being made a curse for us "
(Gal. iii. 13), or " made sin for us " (2 Cor. v. 21).
Lastly, Christ, in the Revelation, is twenty-nine
times spoken of as the Lamb, a title which, whether
it refers to the lamb of the Passover or to the
suffering Servant, represented as a lamb in
Isaiah liii., throws into the foreground the idea of
His sacrificial death. The great vision in the fifth
chapter, of the "Lamb as it had been slain," is
enough to show the depth of the impression made

upon the writer by the Lord's death. Whatever differences there may be as regards outlook and interpretation in the New Testament writers, one could hardly exaggerate the importance to them of the death of Christ. It is in the New Testament first that we find Christian thought agreeing to proclaim in the words of a later writer—*Domini mors potentior erat quam vita :* " the Lord's death was more powerful than His life."

Why that death was so greatly prized we have now seen, also some of the interpretations of it which began almost at once to be made. But so wonderful was the thought—the Lord died for men—so rich and manysided the teaching of the New Testament, that it is no wonder that many different ideas, sometimes leading to almost contrary conclusions, sprang up in the Church and were upheld by great theologians. Such a simple statement as " Christ died for men " gave rise to many questions. What exactly did the " for " imply ? Obviously it meant " for the advantage of men," but did it also mean " instead of men " ? Was Christ in His death the substitute for men ? Again, if it was said that Christ made atonement, in what did the atonement consist ? Did Christ offer some satisfaction to God which the sin of humanity made necessary ; if so, in what did this satisfaction consist ? Or was the atonement a making God and man at one, by showing man how much God had loved him since He had given His Son to die, and by thus arousing in man's heart a love of God and a desire to serve Him ? Then, was the language of the New Testament, the words used by Christ or about

Him, to express the work which He did by His death, to be taken literally ? For instance (and it serves very well to show what difficulties were sure to arise), the Lord had said that He had come " to give His life a ransom for many." In human experience a ransom, whereby some one is released from captivity, is paid to some one. The Lord released man by paying a ransom—to whom ? It may startle us to find that a great many of the ablest theologians of the Church in East and West alike, during the time covered by the third to the twelfth century, replied—to the Devil. For the Devil had certain rights over man, because man had sinned, and therefore if man was to be delivered from the Devil something was due to the Devil in return. But the Devil overreached himself by trying to get into his power Christ, over Whom he had no rights since Christ had not sinned. It was Anselm, the great Archbishop of Canterbury who died in 1109, who was finally, though not immediately, successful in destroying the whole idea of the Devil's rights, and in replacing it by the altogether worthier thought that Christ by His willing acceptance of death, though as sinless He might have avoided it, offered a perfect satisfaction to God for man's sins. Yet this thought also gave rise to many questions. Speaking generally, we may say that the Church did not try to give hard and fast answers to these questions. That Christ died for the salvation of men, that His death had as its effect not simply the arousing of man's love and gratitude but also, and indeed primarily, a perfect satisfaction made to God for the sins of the whole world—this she taught without hesitation. Apart from this she left questions as to the precise reason whereby, the exact way in which, the Lord's death was an atonement for sin, to the schools of theology and her learned divines. There is no great Christian doctrine which has given rise to wider and more varied speculations, none on which the Church has been slower to condemn opinions as heretical.

This is the situation with which we are faced to-day. But it does not at all follow that what a Christian thinks about the death of Christ is unimportant. It is sometimes said, "The *fact* of the Atonement saves us, not the holding of this or that theory about it." This is true enough if it only means that the atoning death can reach to and cover a person who holds no theory at all about it, or even holds an obviously false one. But it is not in the least true if it is intended to imply that it is no great matter what theory a man holds. This is not the case, because, in the first place, some theories are very much more satisfactory than others, and truth, even when it is only a greater degree of truth and not absolute truth, is not a matter of indifference; and, secondly, the fact that "Christ died for men" ought to mean a great deal to a Christian man, and it will mean exceedingly little if he has really no idea of what is implied by those words. Let us see if we cannot advance some little way towards understanding them.

There are two facts in our human life of which we are very conscious—sin and suffering. And these two facts are very closely connected with one another. Suffering is not always, but is exceedingly often, the result of sin, though (and this should be carefully noted) not necessarily the result of the sin of the individual sufferer. Again, suffering, or the punishment which involves suffering, is the right, the just consequence of sin. The words of the penitent thief express this very simply and truly : " We indeed justly [are in the same condemnation]; for we receive the due reward of our deeds." And yet further : suffering can have a purifying effect, and that in two ways. First of all, the person who accepts punishment for sin in the right spirit finds that the suffering has a real power over his sin : it is a purging force, relieving the conscience of the weight of the sin, and strengthening the whole man to meet future temptations. Secondly, suffering, when it is voluntarily accepted, as by the man who is prepared to suffer and die for some great cause, or when it is the suffering of compassion, whereby one person shares in the grief of another, and, as it were, takes over some portion of the weight of that grief, has real moral power. We look on the spirit of self-sacrifice as something specially noble, on sacrificial suffering as worth while, both because of its effect upon the soul of the one who gives himself to some great cause, and because of its influence outside the man himself. In the light of all this let us think of the death of Christ. Christ the incarnate Son of God came to help sinful men. That help took many forms. The fact of the Incarnation was in itself a help, for it showed how ready God was to come to the rescue of men, since He gave His Son to be Man among men. Christ's teaching and miracles of mercy were

another way of help, for they raised men up to a
nobler vision of human life, based on the great
principle of love, and revealed God as the Father
Who cared for the whole man, soul and body.
But beyond all this there was the need that man
should be right with God, that something should
be done to repair all that was wrong in the relations
between God and man on account of sin. God
could not treat sin as anything but sin, could not
simply pass it over, for it was not just a question
of a number of individual sinners, but of mankind
as a whole sinful and guilty (for in a moral world
sin brings guilt with it) in the sight of a holy God.
There was need for some great act of satisfaction
to God made by man, some act of reparation and
atonement, something which should show man
as not only repentant but as willing to suffer the
penalties which his past sin had deserved. Here,
then, is the supreme help which Christ gave. He
was made man, and as man He did for man what
man, apart from Christ, could never have done for
himself, since only the holy can make atonement
to the holy, and man was not holy, but tied and
bound by the chain of his sins. This atonement
Christ wrought in His death, and that for two
reasons,—first, because His life of continual obedience to God's will reached its climax in His death
of perfect obedience to that same will, for He
Himself bears witness that the bitter cup which He
drinks is given Him by the Father (John xvii.
4 ; cf. Matt. xxvi. 39) ; secondly, because in death
He submits to what is not His due. He endures
willingly the sufferings, even up to the last suffering
of death, which are the due reward of sin, and

show God's wrath against sin. He stands where sinners should stand. He has made Himself one with sinful humanity, is identified with it, and so He cannot escape that connection of suffering and penalty with sin which is a law of the moral world ; yet though identified with man He does what sinful man could never do, for His identification with man stops absolutely short of an identification with man's sin. His death is the redeeming act, in virtue, not of the quantity of physical suffering, but of the complete submission of His will to the will of the Father, and the practical acknowledgment, " Thou art righteous that judgest." That acknowledgment brought with it the knowledge through experience of what is called " the pain of loss," that separation of man from God which stands in the first place as God's punishment of sin. The agony in the garden, the cry from the Cross, " My God, My God, why hast Thou forsaken Me ? " show us the incarnate Son entering into that shadow where the brightness of the face of God is withdrawn from man.

And let us remember that all the time God was saving us through and in Christ. God did not desire to destroy man, but to save him. He was not an angry God, Whom only an innocent victim could appease, but the Father Whose holiness could not but react against sin, Whose righteousness could not but ask for some great act of reparation and atonement for sin from humanity, Whose love could not but desire the restoration and salvation of the sinner. So He gave His only Son to be one with man in life and death, to offer a life of perfect obedience and a death of supreme submission, making in humanity's name the great confession, "True and righteous are Thy judgments, O God." So this work pleased God, and for the sake of that work we are accepted " in the Beloved," when we in penitence and faith ask God to look—not at the sins of each one of us, but upon that perfect work which the Perfect Man, the Second Adam, wrought for us. As the hymn says :—

> " Look, Father, look on His anointed face,
> And only look on us as found in Him ;
> Look not on our misusings of Thy grace,
> Our prayer so languid, and our faith so dim :
> For lo ! between our sins and their reward
> We set the Passion of Thy Son, our Lord."

Our Christian prayers, our Christian sacraments, our Christian acts, all look towards that great sacrifice on Calvary. Christians differ as to the way in which the merits, the virtue, of that sacrifice are applied to the soul of the individual sinner for forgiveness and for strength. They do not differ in believing that the Lord's death is the climax of that incarnation, that " humbling Himself " of the Son of God, which was for us men and for our salvation. And so when we say in the Creed, " Suffered under Pontius Pilate, was crucified, dead, and buried," let us remember that this is no unmeaning recitation of a number of historical facts, but that those facts come bringing to us the salvation of our God.

There is but little space to speak of the following words, " He descended into hell." They are words of great comfort : when we think of the dead whom we love so well we ask : " What can we know of that strange country to which they have passed ? " And we answer—it is a country where Christ has been. There is a beautiful hymn by Archbishop Maclagan which imagines for us the joy among the spirits of holy men of old when our Lord came among them. It is not mere imagination ; there is the promise to the dying thief, there is St. Peter's statement that " the gospel was preached also to them that are dead," and we may mention an old tradition which Bishop Irenæus of Lyons, who wrote at the end of the second century A.D., received from a presbyter who had listened to disciples of the Apostles, that Christ, when He descended into Hades, proclaimed there His advent, meaning, doubtless, His incarnation. And so Dr. H. B. Swete has pointed out that it was the privilege of the Church of Aquileia in North Italy, in whose Creed the words first stood, " to hand down to a remote age . . . an apostolic belief which affirms that the Incarnate Son consecrated by His presence the condition of departed souls."

VI

THE RESURRECTION OF JESUS CHRIST

"The third day He rose again from the dead."

WHAT was the Resurrection which the Apostles set themselves to preach ? Why did the fact that they had seen Jesus alive after death assume for them such cardinal significance that it became the core of all their Creed and the end of all their teaching ? Why was it in itself a new Gospel for all mankind ?

We must take their measure of it if we are ever to understand why it is the fundamental and decisive factor in the Christian religion. We must see it with their eyes, and bring to bear upon it their judgment of its values. So only can it become intelligible to us as an inspiration and a life.

For, certainly, to them it was no mere ghost that they had seen returning from the grave, a thin ineffectual phantom hovering on the edge of our earthly frontiers, too frail to count among the solid things that constitute reality. It was no passing vision that came and went and left things as they were. It was no mere assurance that He Who had been dead was alive in some strange other world than this. It was no sudden and solitary miracle that just for once broke the dominion of natural law, and then after this

G

unique interruption left those laws to resume their immemorial routine. It was no unnatural and abnormal wonder out of all context, unrelated, unanticipated, and unexplained.

To them as they gradually apprehended it the Resurrection was the most natural and intelligible and normal fact that had ever occurred. It had been anticipated in every detail of the created life from the beginning of the world; it was the one mystery at the heart of things, the secret up to which everything had led. Through it ran the single purpose into which the Divine Will had laboured to fashion the story of man. Out from it flowed all the force that was to carry on the story to its final consummation.

So it held for them the key to all enigmas. It was the one firm base on which all human existence was built, and far from being a unique breach with natural law, it was itself the very bond by which nature was held together.

That is what it had become as we find it in the Epistles of St. Paul, for instance, who was possessed of one prevailing passion, just to understand and to attain to the resurrection from the dead. Life, he felt, would be all too short to give full value to the central and dominant and inexhaustible manifestation of the creative and redemptive mind of God; for in it, as he believed, lay the solution of every problem, the inspiration of all conduct, the interpretation of all knowledge, and the crown of all desire. So he lived to follow it out and apprehend its fullness and power. So he prayed but one prayer for his children in the faith that " the God of our Lord Jesus Christ, the

Father of glory, may give unto you the spirit of
wisdom and revelation in the knowledge of Him :
the eyes of your understanding being enlightened ;
that ye may know what is the hope of His calling,
and what the riches of the glory of His inheritance
in the saints, and what is the exceeding greatness
of His power to us-ward who believe, according
to the working of His mighty power, which He
wrought in Christ when He raised Him from the
dead " (Eph. i. 17-20).

Now, how had the Resurrection come to mean
all this ? Why did this transcendent miracle
appear to the first disciples to be the one and only
key by which to interpret the entire order of
nature from the beginning of creation ?

Well, first, it was because nature, the natural
order, had been broken to pieces under their eyes.
Just think what they had experienced. They had
learned from their splendid psalms, for instance,
how all nature, in its delicate and seemly order,
moved upward from level to level, through plant
and fish and bird and beast to man, the crowning
act of evolution, " man going forth to his work,
and to his labour until the evening," in the midst
of that busy and harmonious activity of the world.
And out of man God had selected their own people
for special spiritual training—drawn nearer to
God than any other. The God of all the nations
had loved and chosen Zion, that through it He
might declare His Will to all the people on the face
of the earth. And out of Zion there should come
at last the crown of human growth, the consummation of human effort, the Man after God's
own heart, the Anointed, the Beloved. Up to

that consummation all endeavours led, through centuries of travail and discipline and suffering and deliverance.

And at last He had come. He was there in flesh and blood, the Hope of Israel, the Desire of all nations, the Beloved Son, the satisfaction of all the long prayer, the justification of all the painful struggle, the end of all desire : Jesus of Nazareth.

They had lived intimately with Him for some blessed years, and they had seen and touched and handled the Word of Life. They had committed their whole souls to Him ; they had trusted from the very bottom of their hearts that this was He Who should redeem Israel.

And then they had to stand by, powerless and dumb and blind, while the vision was shattered and the hope crushed. Their Life was slain. All that was good and gracious and holy in man had gone under, broken and defeated, beneath the tyranny of evil. And worse. God had made no sign. He had failed His Anointed. There had been no rescue, no deliverance. Hung there on the cursed tree, He, the Blessed One, had fallen under the curse. He had cried aloud to God and had cried in vain. Down the black night fell ; the storm broke. A grim and terrible silence had closed over Him Whose very word had been life. The uttermost disaster had overtaken the one and only hope on which man's whole heart had been staked. There was no more light. Life had ceased to have any purpose in it, any end to propose, any goal to reach. It closed in a supreme act of disillusion, a mad mockery of all that gave it worth and honour and beauty and truth. There was nothing now for them to live for, and nothing to pray for. Nature was emptied of all joy or significance; conscience was wrecked; thought was beggared; love was deceived. Everything that man held dear lay in ruins about them. God's face was hidden; all was lost.

So they lay in the dust on the floor of that Upper Chamber with the doors shut until, according to the most vivid personal record, the light, hurried step of a woman on the stairs bade them open the doors in fear. And the strange news was in their ears: "They have taken away the Lord out of the sepulchre, and we know not where they have laid Him." And Peter ran as he had never run before, and that other disciple ran faster still, and they saw the linen clothes lying, and as they saw, suddenly believed.

And then He was found standing in the midst of them, and saying, "Peace be unto you. Why are ye troubled? Behold My hands and My feet, that is I myself." So the record declares.

And with the vision of the Risen Lord, all life stood upright once again. It was not the mere comfort of knowing Jesus was alive beyond death. But what they saw was this: that God's purpose had never broken; God's will had held true. He had never failed Himself. There had been no withdrawal, no lapse, and no disaster. The pain, the misery, the woe, the agony, the death, had all been leading up to a prepared and purposed close. They had worked towards this end, the Risen Man, the Resurrection from the Dead.

That Risen Man was the culmination of all that man could ever be, the fruit of all his past, the true and proper crown of all his endeavour. In the Risen Christ human history had touched its goal. In Him humanity had won its way to fruition. It had realised its full values. It had attained.

Everything leads up to this, and all becomes coherent again. Bone by bone, as it were, the parts of man came together to build up a perfect body, into which a living spirit has breathed its breath. God has prepared for Himself a Man Who has gathered up into His own Will the entire mass of human desire, the whole varied volume of human experience, and has carried it forward on to a new level, won through death, so that it is now transfigured through and through by the powers of an eternal life in the might of Him Who has filled it with the splendour of His resurrection glory.

All the woeful agony, then, which had seemed to them to be the overthrow of all hope for man, the signal of some moral anarchy, the proof of a devil's triumph, the evidence that all was lost as the Christ went down under the tyranny of evil into the abyss of death—all this was inside the purpose which led to the Resurrection. It was the material through which the purpose passed on to its achievement. It was no blind and stupid disaster. It was part of the Divine counsel, that out of this suffering and death should be wrung the final victory. It had a meaning, and therefore it had been deliberately accepted. The Christ had known it all and bowed His head to it, shrinking indeed from its bitterness, but willing to learn obedience through suffering, and ready to commit Himself to the Father's Will. By this consent it was fired through and through with the spirit of sacrifice. It was changed by this from shame to glory. It was made the one pure and perfect and acceptable offering. It cancelled sin and redeemed humanity. Because He had humbled Himself to a slave's death, the death of a convict upon the Cross, therefore God had highly exalted Him and given Him a name above every name. "He was declared to be the Son of God with power, by the Resurrection from the dead" (Rom. i. 4).

So the great Creed was built up which stretches itself out to embrace the entire drama of man from creation to the end of the world. That drama has found its supreme solution. It can unroll its long story from act to act with an ever-growing consistency of design now that the crisis has come which illuminates the past, and manifests the present, and decrees the future. Given the Resurrection from the dead, all human life is intelligible. So long as you stop short in the natural man, in man under the limitation of mere nature, as a creature of this earth, you have no coherent account to make of him. He arrives at no satisfying end; he is crossed and thwarted by disaster; he finds no adequate fulfilment; his ideals break into fragments; his goal is pushed farther and farther off; his purposes end in vanity; his end is confusion.

And, therefore, this great conclusion is reached: that it is only by the addition of a supernatural outlook that the natural man shows what he is really meant for. Only by seeing this life on earth, so incomplete in itself, as a school for another life beyond death, does this earthly life itself acquire reality and consistency. Only by looking beyond death can death itself become intelligible. Only so can you give any rational value to the sorrow and pain that haunt us here. Only by starting from the resurrection from the dead can you see this life steadily and see it whole.

Now, if this is what the Resurrection meant to the disciples, then it is entirely unique. It has no parallel whatever in history. It is not a mere incident : it contains an entire creed. It is no decorative appendage to a career, which might be possibly omitted without loss to the career itself. Rather, it is the formative and organic secret which gives light and value to everything else. Nothing could be less like it than stories of men who have made so profound an impression for good or evil upon their contemporaries that no one could believe them to be dead, but looked to their coming again. Every form, indeed, of the theory of apotheosis contradicts flatly all the recorded facts. Far from the enthusiastic faith of the disciples sufficing to create the belief in His reappearance after death, their faith had so completely broken down under the blow of the Cross that nothing short of the insistent and irresistible impact of the fact could avail to recreate it. Moreover, there was no material in their minds out of which a suggestion of what we have described could emerge. The Old Testament has nothing that in the least corresponds to the complex idea

which the Resurrection embodied. The records
of our Lord's life tell us frankly enough that even
when our Lord reiterated the word Resurrection
in their ears they never took it in. It conveyed
nothing positive to them. And the Agony of the
Cross, when it fell upon them, obliterated, it
would seem, every memory of what might have
given them some vague comfort in the crisis. It
is extraordinarily convincing that they should
themselves report their own total lack of understanding at the time.

And then there is nothing that even attempts
to account for the entire change in the disciples
from men of dull and distressing impotence in the
Gospels to men of amazing courage, insight, and
resolution in the Acts, except the reality of the
fact that the Lord had risen to a life of energy
and power by the force of which fact they were
seized from without, and over-mastered, and transformed. On any other hypothesis, this miraculous
transformation of character remains wholly inexplicable.

And it is this signal transformation which He,
the Lord as risen, has power to work through the
Spirit on all who believe in Him, which would
always be the best and final evidence of the fact
that He rose again. The existence of the Christian
Church is the only proof of the Resurrection that
we now can verify in our own experience. The
historical evidence for the fact is of singular force ;
but it is, of course, subject to all the limitations
that are bound to beset the historical evidence
for very remote facts. Such evidence can never
be absolute. The impression it produced must be

subject to every variety of temperament; and will depend for its convincing force on all kinds of presuppositions in the mind of the person to whom the proof is offered. In this particular case, the evidence bears the mark of validity, of reality, just because, while it is unwavering in its assertion of the actual fact, it nevertheless has not attempted to harmonise the incidental fluctuations and contradictions of the several witnesses. It has candidly left these unsolved. That the Body was gone and the Tomb empty they one and all assert without a doubt; and about this pains are taken to show how complete and reliable is the witness. For it was the very women who had seen where exactly it was laid who go to the same spot to find it gone. That the Lord was seen by His disciples in a bodily form, which was indeed changed from its old conditions so that at first they hardly recognised it, yet which had an essential identity of character with the Body which had been His in His earthly life, and made Him still to be the very Man whom they had known —on this they are one and all positively agreed. But in what exact order of time the various visions were seen, and why it was that the visions should be promised them in Galilee and then, after all, occur mainly in Jerusalem, they did not attempt to explain. This fixed agreement on the fact, combined with uncertainty in details, corresponds precisely with what we should expect, if the tale were undoubtedly true. Take an instance. When Samuel Wilberforce, the famous Bishop of Winchester, fell from his horse and broke his neck in a Surrey woodland, Sir Thomas Farrer and his servants were hastily summoned from the cricket-ground, where they were playing, to pick up his body and carry it to Abinger House, where Sir Thomas lived. They were greatly moved by the sudden tragedy, and the incident was deeply imprinted in their memories. Yet, on the very next day, when they were asked to guide Pressmen to the spot, they could not agree as to where exactly it was: and when the time came for placing a memorial Cross, no reconciliation of the various statements was found possible, and the only thing to be done was to accept Sir Thomas Farrer's verdict as master of the house. Yet this uncertainty of impression was consistent with the absolute certainty that there on that ground they had found the body and had carried it home. This little parallel may serve to show how entirely the evidence for the Resurrection corresponds to the type which such evidence will naturally take. It is as good evidence as you could wish of its kind; but the proofs that convince the soul must always be of another type. They cannot belong to that order of evidence which would count in a law court. They must be themselves alive with spiritual energy. They must be the outcome of the fact itself, so that the fact carries with it its own evidence by virtue of its own inherited self-verification. The Resurrection must prove itself by that which it does. It has shown itself as an operative cause of great power on the stage of human history. We can follow its work amidst scenery that we know and understand, until it arrives down the centuries at our own immediate date, and presses itself in upon our own experience.

According to what it has proved itself, and can still prove itself to be, we shall be persuaded to believe it really happened.

And if it can so verify itself to us as a real and effective actuality, then we shall accept the account of those who were its immediate witnesses for the form in which it actually manifested itself to them. We have surely no choice about this. They alone saw and heard. They alone had been selected and equipped for this very purpose by the Master, that they might become witnesses of His Resurrection. They had companioned with Him from the baptism of John till His death. They ate and drank with Him after He rose from the dead. They felt His breath upon them in the Upper Chamber. They saw the wounds in His hands. And, moreover, they held together, in a single unbroken nucleus, for twenty or thirty years in order to deliver this their witness in the very spot where the Body had been buried and had disappeared—the very spot where their tale could be best challenged and disproved if it were not true. They never left that spot of witness until the invading hosts, gathering for the destruction of Jerusalem, drove them perforce off the ground. Such was their deliberate, organised and concerted evidence, which they set themselves to deliver and to secure from the first moment of the Church's existence. And what it was that they so asserted we know from the primitive records of St. Peter's earliest speeches in the Acts, and from the fixed tradition to which St. Paul appeals in the fifteenth chapter of the First Epistle to the Corinthians, as well as from the allusions which he makes to what was common ground to all believers in the Resurrection. It is clear that they themselves believed that What had died and been buried rose again. What was the nature of the change worked upon it they did not attempt to define ; but that which had been His Body in the days of the flesh they believed to be His Body still ; only it had become a Spiritual Body, a Body, that is, raised to a spiritual level, a perfect organ of spirit, qualified to live the life of spirit ; but still a Body, a Sacrament of the Spirit, an outward expression of an inward spiritual reality, with some identity of structure and function with what it had been. In it and by it Christ was recognised as having taken with Him into the new life all that had made Him a real Man while He was here, all that had identified His nature with ours, all that had been manifested to men on earth in terms of flesh and blood. He was still, after death, the Jesus Whom John had seen and touched and loved ; on Whose breast he had lain ; the Jesus Whose eyes had read men's souls and Whose voice had been in their ears, and Whose hands had healed. That Manhood of His which had gone down to death was recovered and retained ; and still His life in the Spirit would come to them in a form which it was right to speak of as a Body broken and as Blood shed. Still there was a Body of His of which, now, they all became members, and which was so verily akin to our own bodily nature that it became an everlasting pledge that He Who had raised our souls from the death of sin would finally quicken also our mortal bodies by the Spirit that dwelleth in us, so that even now on earth the body may become dead to its sin and we may present it a living sacrifice, holy and acceptable unto God.

This was the Gospel delivered by St. Paul—a Gospel which was not of his own making, for he had received it—how that Christ died for our sins according to the Scriptures, and was buried, and rose again on the third day. He Whose Body was buried rose again. It was sown a natural Body; it was raised a Spiritual Body. And in it He was seen of Cephas, then of the Twelve, after that of about five hundred brethren at once, of whom some remained and some had fallen asleep; after that of James; and then last of all of Paul—for whom life had henceforth but one purpose and but one desire, that he might himself attain unto the Resurrection from the Dead.

VII

THE ASCENSION OF JESUS CHRIST

" He ascended into heaven, and sitteth on the right hand of God the Father Almighty."

"THE third day He rose again from the dead; He ascended into heaven, And sitteth on the right hand of God the Father Almighty." These three articles in that section of the Apostles' Creed which refers to our Lord Jesus Christ are closely related. It is the second and the third of them which we have now to consider. The article which deals with the Ascension is an acknowledgment of our belief in an event which we assign to the sphere of history as having once taken place on earth. On the other hand, the article which deals with the Lord's Session at the right hand of God is an acknowledgment of our belief in a fact which belongs to the unseen and divine world, and which, therefore, we assign to the sphere of theology. The historical event is the basis of the theological fact. For the Church has always regarded the Ascension as an assurance that the Lord Jesus Christ, Who was truly born, Who truly died, and Who truly rose the third day from the dead, now truly " sitteth on the right hand of God the Father Almighty."

There are two matters which seem to lie on the

threshold of our subject; and for the sake of clearness it is well at the beginning to say a word about each of them.

(1) We are conscious that there are two worlds. There is the world of phenomena, the world of time and of place, in which we are, and which we think that we know. There is also the world of final realities, apart from time and apart from space, to which belong God and the things of God, and to apprehend which we have no faculties given to us. The revelation of God in our Lord Jesus Christ pertains to the world of time and of place; under the conditions of time and of place it was wrought out; and in language limited by those conditions the record of that revelation has come to us. It is not without cause that we remind ourselves of this elementary truth. For we are sometimes tempted in our thoughts about the Lord's manifestation on earth to endeavour to make a brief and sudden excursion into that other world of final realities which lies wholly beyond our powers to conceive and to contemplate; and the outcome of that fruitless endeavour is confusion and perplexity. But specially do we need to be on our guard against this temptation when we are dealing with the Resurrection, and the Ascension. For these events (as we believe them to be) lie on the frontier of the two worlds. We may well think that in them, if we could grasp their final interpretation, we should find that we have a reconciliation of the antithesis between the two worlds, the world of phenomena and the world of final reality. Yet it remains certain that, while we are what we are, we must be

content to think and speak of these supreme events in terms of time and place.

(2) What is the relation of the Resurrection and the Ascension of our Lord ? In speaking of the subject we are brought at once into the region of modern controversies. On the one hand, the tendency of much recent criticism and thought is to deny that there was an Ascension of the Lord distinct from the Resurrection, and to explain the Resurrection itself not as a definite event but rather as an assurance, conveyed to the disciples by means of visions, that their Master had survived death and was with God. On the other hand, the faith of the Universal Church, expressed in the Creeds, is (if I may venture to translate it into my own words) that all the elements of the Lord's humanity were preserved in death and raised from death, so transfigured that they were brought into a true unity and perfectness corresponding to the spiritual order into which He had now passed ; and that the historical event of a true Resurrection was after an interval followed by the historical event of a true Ascension. At the same time it must be fully recognised that as a matter of history it was the Resurrection which changed the Apostles and their companions and which thus became the birthday of the Christian Church (comp., *e.g.*, 1 Peter i. 3), and further, that, as the coronation of a monarch is implied in his accession, so (if the analogy may be permitted) the Ascension was involved in the Resurrection. When the Lord appeared to His disciples on that third day, He had already ceased to be subject to the laws which

H

govern man's life on earth; already He had entered on a mode of being which was divine. He came indeed to His followers; but He came to them as a visitor from a higher world. For Him glory had already taken the place of humiliation (comp. Phil. iii. 21). Thus the Ascension confirmed and enlarged rather than originated the disciples' conviction as to their Master's exaltation. In a true sense we may conceive of the Ascension as an event subordinate to the Resurrection. We must not be surprised if the latter, as compared with the former, holds a position primary and supreme in the teaching of the Apostolic Church.

In the Creed we confess our belief in the Ascension of our Lord as an event distinct from His Resurrection. An alleged historical event can be established only by an appeal to results caused by it and by an appeal to testimony. It must be conceded at once that the results of the Ascension cannot be separated from the results of the Resurrection. Together they explain the origin of the Christian Church. But, as we have just seen, the Resurrection dominated early Christian thought; and if it were maintained that the great issue was due to the Resurrection alone, there could be no proof to the contrary. We turn therefore to the question of testimony.

If any one examines a collection of Christian Creeds, he will see for himself that the Creeds of the East and of the West alike contain articles of faith in the Resurrection of the Lord on the third day, in the Ascension, in the Session at the right hand of God. It is needless to labour this point.

But there is an earlier stage in the history of the confessions of the Christian faith of which account must be taken. I refer to those creed-like statements of belief in writers of the second century, in some of which, if not in all, we catch echoes of very early Creeds, or at least see Creeds in process of formation. These Creed-like statements meet us in the Tracts of Tertullian of Carthage (*circ.* A.D. 190–215), in the controversial Treatise of Irenæus (*circ.* A.D. 175–190), in Justin Martyr's Apologies on behalf of the Christians addressed to the Heathen and to the Jews (*circ.* A.D. 140–160), and in the Apology of Aristides (*circ.* A.D. 125–130) addressed to the Emperor Hadrian. Of such passages two specimens will suffice. Irenæus was born in Asia Minor, where he was the pupil of Polycarp of Smyrna (himself the pupil of St. John) ; he lived and taught in Rome ; and later he became Bishop of Lyons in South Gaul. Thus Irenæus is a link between different generations and between widely separated regions. In his "Treatise against Heresies" (I. 10 1 *f.*, ed. Massuet) he insists that the Church, "scattered throughout the whole world, even unto the ends of the earth," "carefully preserves as though she dwelt in one single house" the faith which she "received from the Apostles and from their disciples." And in his setting forth of this faith there occur the words, "the passion and the resurrection from the dead and the assumption in the flesh into heaven of the Beloved, even Christ Jesus our Lord." Again, Aristides tells the Emperor that "the Christians are reckoned in descent from the Lord Jesus Christ," and then records the Christians' faith about their

Founder : " Through the Cross, of His own free will and counsel, He tasted death according to a mighty dispensation ; and after three days He revived and went up into heaven." The testimony, then, to this article of the Creed—" He ascended into heaven "—so universal, so early, so clear, is a strong indication that it was part, if we may use the expression, of the original deposit ; that, in other words, it came to the Churches of the second century through the many streams which flowed from that watershed of Christian thought and teaching, the Apostolic age.

Is this conclusion verified by a study of the documents of the New Testament ? For the purposes of the brief review which follows I have arranged the Books of the New Testament in groups. This arrangement must not be taken as implying a decisive judgment on questions of date and authorship—*e.g.*, the question of the later date (*circ.* A.D. 95) or the earlier date (*circ.* A.D. 68) of the Apocalypse, and the question whether the author of the Apocalypse is the author of the Fourth Gospel.

(1) *The Johannine Books :*

(*a*) The Gospel : vi. 62 ; vii. 39 ; xiv. 2 *f.*, 28 ; xv. 26 ; xvi. 7, 28 ; xx. 17 (where the Lord is represented on the morning of the Resurrection as implying His future Ascension and as speaking of His Resurrection-life as involving the Ascension —" I ascend ").

(*b*) The First Epistle : The words, " We have an advocate with the Father, Jesus Christ the righteous " (ii. 1), imply the idea of the Lord's return to, and close communion with, the Father.

(c) The Apocalypse: xii. 5 (where the woman travailing appears to signify the Church of Israel, the child born of her to signify the Messiah; it is added: " and her child was caught up unto God and unto His throne "). For the Session, see iii. 21 and (under different imagery) v. 6; vii. 17; xxii. 3.

(2) *The First Epistle of St. Peter :* iii. 21 *f.* " through the resurrection of Jesus Christ; who is on the right hand of God, having gone into heaven " (where the mention of the Resurrection, the journey into heaven, and the Session will be noticed); comp. i. 21 (where the words " and gave him glory " naturally, though not necessarily, refer to the Ascension).

(3) *The Epistle to the Hebrews :* It would hardly be an exaggeration to say that the theme of this Epistle is *the Gospel of the Ascension.* This " Gospel " meets us not in isolated allusions; it is rather written large over the whole letter. For at the heart of its teaching lies the parallel between the many High Priests of Israel and the one High Priest of the human race, " Jesus, the Son of God." The successive High Priests on the Day of Atonement offered the sacrifice and then passed through the veil and with the blood of the sacrifice entered into the Holy of Holies. The Lord Jesus offered Himself and then " passed through the heavens " (iv. 14) " into heaven itself, now to appear before the face of God for us " (ix. 24). The Ascension is the centre of the theology of this Book. Moreover, characteristic emphasis is also laid on the thought of the Session (i. 3; viii. 1; x. 12; xii. 2); and in two of the four passages just referred to

(viii. 1; x. 12) this image of kingly dignity is added to the image of High Priestly ministration. A review of the teaching of this Epistle justifies two assertions. First, such an interpretation as this writer gives to the Ascension is obviously the outcome of protracted thought. The Ascension as a great event must long have been before his mind. In the second place, he clearly assumes a knowledge of the Ascension on the part of his readers. He could not hope to help them by his own mystic thoughts unless he was assured that the basis of fact on which he built up his thoughts was familiar to them.

(4) *The Pauline Epistles :*

(*a*) The Pastoral Epistles : The one passage in these Epistles which contains a reference to the Ascension is a quotation. Two primitive Christian hymns are cited in the New Testament. It is remarkable that the inspiration of the first (Eph. v. 14) is the Resurrection of Christ, while the climax of the second, adduced in 1 Tim. iii. 16, is the Ascension of Christ—" He was received up in glory." Again we infer that the Ascension was a matter of common knowledge to the Christians of those days.

(*b*) The Epistles of the first Captivity : The Epistle to the Ephesians is of special importance in regard to our present inquiry. In it St. Paul sets forth his doctrine of the Church and of the relation of the Church to the Person of Christ. Here, then, we should expect to find clear references to the Ascension and the Session ; and our expectation is not disappointed. In i. 20 *f.* the Session is spoken of as a stage in the exaltation

of Christ distinct from, and subsequent to, the
Resurrection (comp. ii. 6). And if it is urged that
the Ascension itself had no place in the writer's
thoughts about the regnant Christ, a later passage
in the Epistle supplies the seeming deficiency. In
iv. 8 *ff.* the Apostle applies to Christ the words of
Ps. lxviii. 18, " Thou hast ascended on high." The
testimony of these sayings is clear and explicit.
But the witness of the Epistle to the acknowledgment by the Apostle and his correspondents of the
Ascension and the Session does not depend on
particular phrases. They together constitute an
axiom without which the characteristic teaching
of the Epistle would have been impossible. In the
other Epistles of this group the following passages
will repay careful study : Col. iii. 1 *ff.* ; Phil. ii.
9 *ff.* ; iii. 20 *f.*

(c) The Epistles of Paul the Traveller : In the
Epistle to the Romans two passages stand out.
In viii. 34 (" It is Christ Jesus that died, yea
rather, that was raised from the dead, Who is at
the right hand of God, Who also maketh intercession for us ") the abiding fact of the Session is
mentioned as distinct from the event of the Resurrection. In Rom. x. 6 *ff.* we have a mystical
rabbinic exposition of the words of Deut. xxx.
12 *ff.* which may well seem foreign to our modern
ways of thinking ; but to me at least this is clear,
that, on the one hand, no one could have written
that comment (" Who shall descend into the abyss?
(that is, to bring Christ up from the dead) ") who
did not know that Christ had died and been buried
(comp. 1 Cor. xv. 3) ; and, on the other hand, no
one could have written that comment (" Who

shall ascend into heaven ? (that is, to bring Christ down) ") who did not know that Christ had ascended into heaven. In the First Epistle to the Corinthians the words, "when He shall deliver up the kingdom to God, even the Father," and " for He must reign, till He hath put all enemies under His feet " (xv. 24 *f.*), imply a belief in Christ's Session at the right hand of God. This belief, indeed, is the whole content of that brief formula " Jesus is Lord " which there is good ground for regarding as the primitive Christian Creed (1 Cor. xii. 3 ; Rom. x. 9 ; comp. *e.g.* 1 Cor. viii. 6 ; Phil. ii. 11 ; Acts ii. 36). Finally there is in this group of Epistles a series of eschatological passages which appear to postulate an Ascension of our Lord into heaven and His Session there as King. These are 1 Thess. iv. 16 (" The Lord Himself shall descend from heaven "); v. 23; 2 Thess. i. 7; ii. 1 ; 2 Cor. i. 14; v. 10.

As we review the testimony of the Epistles we must remember two of their characteristics. (1) Their references to the events which belong to the historic faith of the Church are incidental and not systematic ; and the events of the Lord's life to which allusion is made are strangely few. (2) Their references to these few events are bare of details. How little do we learn from the Epistles as to the circumstances even of the Lord's death or of His Resurrection !

We now turn to the Synoptic Gospels and the Acts. From the other Books of the New Testament we have gathered such evidence as we had a right to expect from them that the early

Apostolic Churches believed in the Lord's Session at the right hand of God (the source of their phraseology being Ps. cx. 1) and in *an* Ascension of the Lord into heaven.

The First Gospel closes with the notice of a meeting between the risen Lord and the disciples in Galilee, and with a record of words spoken by the Lord which clearly looked forward to a final parting.

The Second Gospel abruptly breaks off with a statement about the women on the morning of the Resurrection—"for they were afraid" (xvi. 8). The present ending of this Gospel belongs probably to the period which immediately succeeded the age of the Apostles. It is largely a compilation from the Canonical Gospels, and is valuable as a witness to what was known and thought by Christians in the early years probably of the second century. Its words are distinct : " So then the Lord Jesus, after He had spoken unto them, was received up into heaven and sat down at the right hand of God."

It must, then, be candidly admitted that the narrative of the Ascension rests on the authority of a single writer, the author of the Third Gospel and of the Acts. There seems to be no reason to question, and there are several considerations which confirm, the very early traditional view which identifies this writer with St. Luke. If we accept this identification, and if we would estimate the value of St. Luke's authority as an historian, we must remember two facts. (1) St. Luke was the friend and companion of St. Paul (comp. Col. iv. 14 ; 2 Tim. iv. 11 ; and the so-called "we"

passages of the Acts—*i.e.* xvi. 10–16; xx. 5–xxviii.
16) ; and St. Paul some five to eight years after
the Ascension spent a fortnight at Jerusalem with
Cephas and James (Gal. i. 18 *f.*), and fourteen years
later met St. John also at Jerusalem (Gal. ii. 1, 9).
(2) St. Luke himself, as we learn from the Acts
(xxi. 15 *ff.*), some quarter of a century after the
Ascension visited Jerusalem with St. Paul and
became known to St. James and to the Elders of
the Church there, some at least among whom must
have seen and heard the Lord ; and during at any
rate part of St. Paul's two years' imprisonment at
Cæsarea St. Luke was in Palestine. Thus, partly
through his own intercourse with some of them,
partly indirectly through his friendship with St.
Paul, St. Luke was brought into contact with those
who were primary witnesses to the great facts of
the Gospel.

The narrative of the Ascension in the Gospel
according to St. Luke (xxiv. 50 *ff.*) is very brief,
but is singularly impressive : " While he blessed
them, he parted from them, and was carried up
into heaven." Two points, however, must be
considered. (1) It is urged that there is no break
in the narrative, and that therefore St. Luke places
the Ascension on the evening of the day of the
Resurrection, and thus contradicts what he himself
says of the forty days in Acts i. 3. Of this objection
it must suffice here to say that it is obvious that on
this last page of his Gospel St. Luke is giving a
rapid summary of events ; and further that elsewhere he records sayings of Christ without defining
their relation to the preceding context (see *e.g.* xii.
54; xiii. 6; xvi. 1), and that therefore we are justified

in thinking that the words "And he said unto them" (*v.* 44) introduce a new scene, and preface sayings which were spoken at a later time than the evening of the first Easter day.* (2) The Revised Version has the marginal note: "Some ancient authorities omit *and was carried up into heaven.*" The question raised by this note obviously cannot be discussed here. It may, however, be said with some confidence that the "ancient authorities" referred to are remarkable for their omissions as well as for their additions of words and clauses.† If these words are omitted, all mention of an Ascension is, of course, eliminated, while yet the whole solemn context and the position of the narrative at the very close of the treatise indicate that the writer is recording what he knows to be a final parting. But the opening paragraph of the Acts includes in the scope of the "first treatise" all that Jesus did and taught "until the day in which he was received up." To most minds this

---

* A passage in the so-called Epistle of Barnabas (xv. 9) is often quoted as affirming that the Ascension took place on the day of the Resurrection. It runs thus : "Wherefore also we keep the eighth day for rejoicing, in which Jesus did both rise from the dead and, when He had manifested Himself, went up into heaven." The passage therefore rather asserts that the Resurrection and the Ascension took place on different Sundays.

† It is perhaps right to say that I discussed this question in a book— *The Syro-Latin Text of the Gospels*—published some twenty years ago. I there offered an explanation of the omission which I believe to be at least worthy of serious consideration. As the matter is an important one, I venture to quote what I then wrote (p. 131 *n.*) : "The reading of the Sinaitic Old Syriac text explains how the omission in the Western texts may have arisen. It has : 'And–when He blessed them, *He–was–lifted–up* from–*them.*' Here plainly the Syriac has a compressed rendering of the two clauses 'He parted from them, and was carried up into heaven,' the ideas being preserved, the phraseology abbreviated. A copyist, however, assimilating the Greek to this old Syriac text would naturally be led by the Syriac reading to omit the words 'and was carried up into heaven.'"

will appear a conclusive argument for the position that the closing words of the Gospel are a record of the Ascension.*

When from the Gospel we pass to the Acts we are confronted with no such questions as those with which we have just dealt. The narrative of the last interview between the Lord and the disciples reaches its climax in the words (*v.* 9) : " And when he had said these things, as they were looking, he was taken up ; and a cloud received him out of their sight." We are so familiar with the passage that we are hardly conscious of its wonderful simplicity and restraint. The central Greek word —" he was taken up "—is derived from the story of Elijah's passing from earth (2 Kings ii. 9 *ff.* ; comp. Ecclus. xlviii. 9) ; but the contrast between the description of the Ascension of the Lord and that of the ascension of Elijah is very great. There is nothing in the former to correspond to the " chariot of fire and horses of fire " and " the whirlwind " of the latter. The story is bare of any details which can justly be called mythical. The difficulty which it presents is essentially the same as the difficulty presented by the appearances and disappearances of the risen Lord recorded in the Gospels. If we grant that after the Resurrection our Lord's body was (to use St. Paul's paradox) a " spiritual body," we have the key to a mystery which lies outside our present experience.

* I have for a long time held, for purely literary reasons, that St. Luke wrote the Acts first and then the Gospel. When they were published, this order was necessarily reversed. I cherish the hope that some time I may be able to publish my reasons for this opinion. If it is sound, it obviously removes all difficulty in the relation of the story of the Ascension in the Gospel to that in the Acts. In the Gospel St. Luke tells briefly what he has already told at length.

The allusions to *an* Ascension of the Lord found in the other books of the New Testament imply a knowledge of such a history as we actually find in the two Lucan Books, or (if we still have any lingering doubts as to the significance of the closing verses of the Gospel) at least in the first chapter of the Acts. Such allusions require a justification : they receive a justification from the witness of St. Luke. There is doubtless more cogent evidence that the Lord did ascend than there is for the particular story of the Ascension which comes to us on the authority, tested as it is in many ways and approved, of the one historian. But it is not too much to say that the confession of the Creeds, the credal statements of Christian writers in the second century, the allusions in the New Testament, and, lastly, the story told us by St. Luke, are strictly in harmony with each other, and that together they form a solid and stable whole.

It is now time that we should ask ourselves what (so far as our minds can apprehend) is the true character of the Ascension and what the true significance of the Session of the Lord Jesus at the right hand of God.

It is probably impossible for us in our study of the *momenta* of the Lord's incarnate life to discern with anything like absolute accuracy what element in each is essential to it in its proper character and what element is (so to speak) superimposed that the whole transaction may be a revelation to men and speak to men in terms which they can understand. But we can hardly be greatly in error if we say that that which was outward and visible in the Ascension—the Lord was raised from the earth and hidden from view by the encircling cloud —was not for His sake but for the sake of the Apostles and of those who should believe through their word. In no other way so far as we can see could the Apostles have been taught that their Master was for ever truly man, but that the days of His humiliation were now over and that henceforth He was with the Father. For in truth "upwards" and "downwards," "ascent" and "descent," are terms relative to our common apprehension of things. The heaven which is above our heads is underneath the feet of our fellow-citizens in Australia. Let us—for in these things we are all children—make our appeal to the devotional language of children.

> "There's a Friend for little children
> Above the bright blue sky."

To the little child the words suggest a clear image of the majesty and purity and blessedness in which God ever is. But the words are a necessary accommodation. We know that the Friend is not seated in a mysterious palace somewhere in space, but is at the little child's side, within the little child's heart, yet of infinite greatness and power and love. So, when we contemplate the Ascension we must guard ourselves against resting in any conception of a physical elevation as in itself a final and absolute truth. We may, I believe, fearlessly accept the Ascension (such an Ascension as is recorded by St. Luke) as an historical event, and find in the historical event a parable unfolding to us men a spiritual and divine truth about the Lord Jesus Christ.

What the Church believes that spiritual and divine truth to be is expressed in the confession— He " sitteth on the right hand of God the Father Almighty." Yet still the truth is set forth in a parable, but a parable not now of action but of words. The phrase, as we have already seen, is derived from what was written aforetime about the majesty and honour to which the son of the King of Israel was exalted. Already, it would seem probable, before our Lord appealed to the Psalm as He was teaching in the Temple (Mark xii. 35 *f.*), the words had been invested with a meaning nobler and more sacred than that which belongs to anything of royal splendour. Their Messianic associations prepared them for the use to which the earliest preachers of the Gospel put them (comp. Acts ii. 34; Col. iii. 1; Eph. i. 20; Heb. i. 13; viii. 1; x. 12; xii. 2). If we try to draw out the meaning of the parable in its new and highest context we shall probably agree that four great ideas are shadowed forth in it. These are a return to God; rest; leadership; sovereignty.

A return to God. So we must speak who can view the Incarnation only from its earthly side. The Incarnation to us seems to have broken for a time the perfect union and communion between the eternal Father and the eternal Son. To us therefore the Ascension appears to restore what "for us men and for our salvation" had been taken away.

Rest. Weariness, pain, " acquaintance with grief," proximity to sin, nay whatever of humilia-

tion might seem to linger still about the risen
Christ when from time to time He appeared to
His disciples in the likeness of a man—all this was
openly declared to have been abolished for ever
when the Lord's Ascension set its seal to the Lord's
Resurrection. He is true man still; but He is
glorified.

Leadership. Christ in His Resurrection was
" the firstfruits " (1 Cor. xv. 20). There is some
true sense in which He is " the first fruits " in His
Ascension also, though we shrink from any attempt
to give a clear and definite shape to the thought.
But in many ways it finds expression in the New
Testament : " I go to prepare a place for you.
And if I go and prepare a place for you, I come
again, and will receive you unto myself; that
where I am, there ye may be also " (John xiv.
2 *f.*) ; " Who shall fashion anew the body of our
humiliation, that it may be conformed to the body
of his glory " (Phil. iii. 21); " Whither as a fore-
runner Jesus entered for us " (Heb. vi. 20) ; " He
that overcometh, I will give to him to sit down
with me in my throne, as I also overcame, and
sat down with my Father in his throne " (Rev.
iii. 21). Christ in His Ascension reveals the
destiny of those who are " in Christ."

Sovereignty. This last idea has two aspects.
(1) Some of the profoundest thoughts of the New
Testament gather round the conception of the
divine Word. As the divine Word Christ is " the
light of men," the Tutor of all, to use an image
familiar in early Christian literature, so that every
fragment of truth to which men cling, every
aspiration, social and personal, which makes for

righteousness and charity and reverence, are not the product of their own unaided powers but are the very inspiration of the Word. Again, the Apostles, in words which at least from some points of view can be understood better to-day than when they were first written, unfold to us the mysterious thought that through the eternal Word all things were made, that in Him they are and in Him move onward towards their appointed goal (comp. Col. i. 15 *ff*.; Heb. i. 2 *f*.; John i. 1 *ff*.). Now we may not think that these offices of the Eternal Word were suspended when He became flesh and dwelt as man among men. He was still the Word sown in the hearts and consciences of men, still the sustainer and goal of the universe. But in the days of His earthly sojourn, as we look on the picture of the Son of Man drawn for us in the Gospels, we can see only the signs of His self-emptying, of His lowliness, of His humble obedience even to the last issue of human weakness. It *seems* to us that during those years of earthly life and ministry the Lord's work in the universe and in the world of men must have been intermitted. The Ascension reassures us. When by an outward and visible act He left the world and went to the Father, He made it possible for His disciples to believe that essentially and eternally He bears on all things, all things in the sphere of human life, all things in the sphere of the world of nature, to their destined consummation. So we get a glimpse into the meaning of St. Paul's paradox (Eph. iv. 10): "He . . . ascended far above all the heavens, that he might fill all things" (comp. i. 23). (2) The thought of the Lord's supremacy

I

in the world of grace is in some sort familiar to us.
In that great passage in which St. Paul unfolds
the mystery of Christ the immediate sequel of the
words " He raised him from the dead and made
him to sit at his right hand in the heavenly places"
is found in the words "And gave him to be head
over all things to the Church" (Eph. i. 20 *ff.*).
We are living in " the days " (Matt. xxviii. 20) of
the heavenly ministry of the Lord Jesus Christ.
Our conception of that ministry includes all our
thoughts about the present relation of the Lord
Jesus Christ to all the members of His Body.
But the truths which belong to a confession of His
sovereignty in the Church are set forth in the
later section of the Creed and demand separate
treatment. It is enough for us, if it may have
been so, to penetrate a little way into the meaning
of the Church's eucharistic hymn :

" Thou only art holy ; Thou only art the Lord ;
Thou only, O Christ, with the Holy Ghost, art
most high in the glory of God the Father."

VIII

JESUS CHRIST AS JUDGE

"From thence He shall come to judge the quick and the dead."

THE world has not seen the last of Jesus
Christ our Lord. He "was crucified,
dead, and buried"; but "the third day He
rose again." He "ascended into heaven, and
sitteth on the right hand of God"; but "from
thence He shall come to judge" mankind. All
human history from the first appearance of man
upon the earth until the Incarnation was a preparation for His first coming; all human history
from the Ascension to this day has been a preparation for His Return. In "the fulness of the
time" God "sent forth His Son, born of a woman."
When the time is full again, He will send Him
forth again in the glory of the Father. "We
believe that Thou shalt come to be our Judge."

We speak of two comings of our Lord. There
have been, and there are, many comings of the
Son of God to the world. We believe that the
Eternal Word came forth from the bosom of
the Father to create. All things were made through
Him, things on earth and things in heaven, things
visible and invisible. The true Light which
lighteth every man is ever entering human life.
Life, so far as it is progress, is the growing manifestation of His presence. In an especial manner

He came to His own people Israel, guiding and shaping their national life by law and prophecy. That Israel disregarded His voice, that the world He had made failed to recognise His Presence, does not lessen the wonder of the fact. To the Church, the new Israel, He comes still by His Spirit, in His Sacraments, in the life of the Body and of each of its true members. But of the many comings of our Lord two stand out pre-eminently, and from the earliest Christian times these have been known as the First and Second Advents :* the coming in the flesh and the coming in glory. It is the latter of these in which Jesus Christ will be manifested as Judge.

Of a glorious Return our Lord spoke freely and often during the later months of His ministry in Galilee. He began to speak of it as soon as He began to speak of His approaching death—that is, just before the Transfiguration. " From that time," as we read in St. Matthew (xvi. 21), " began Jesus to shew unto His disciples how that He must be killed, and the third day be raised up." But He did not stop there. " The Son of Man," He added, apparently on the same occasion, " shall come in the glory of His Father, with His angels, and then shall He render unto every man according to his deeds."† Thenceforth the thought of His Return finds frequent expression in our Lord's utterances, especially in the parables. The Good Samaritan will repay what is spent for him, when he comes back again (Luke x. 35). The disciples

---

* See Justin's *Dialogue*, 52.

† This saying is reported in almost identical words by the three Synoptists (Matt. xvi. 27 ; Mark viii. 38 ; Luke viii. 26).

are to be as men who look for their Lord when He
shall return from His journey (Luke xii. 36) ; as
virgins that go forth to meet the bridegroom ; as
servants, who when the master comes back will be
called to account for their use of the talents
entrusted to them (Matt. xxv. 1-12, 14-30). We
even have a vivid description of the judgment
scene, which represents the Son of Man as sitting on
His throne, with all the nations gathered round
Him to receive His award of life or death (Matt.
xxv. 31-46). St. Matthew places this scene immediately before the history of the Passion, and
it is clear from other Synoptic references to the
Return that the Lord's mind dwelt increasingly
upon it as the time of His death drew near. When
the Return should take place, whether it should
follow immediately after His departure or be long
delayed, is not made clear ; the time of the Advent
did not lie within His human knowledge (Mark xiii.
32). But that it should come, sooner or later, He
had no doubt ; the second coming was as certain
to Him as the crucifixion and the rising from the
dead.

Such sayings may have been little understood
at the time by those who heard them, but after the
Ascension they were remembered, and their significance was realised. Even as He ascended, a
vision of angels turned the thoughts of the Eleven
to His coming again. As the days went on, this
hope expressed itself in glowing words which sought
to describe the scene of the Return. " The Lord
Himself," writes St. Paul in one of his earliest
Epistles, " shall descend from heaven with a shout,
with the voice of the archangel and with the trump

of God" (1 Thess. iv. 16). "Behold," exclaims
the prophet of the Apocalypse, in the last years of
the first century, "He cometh with clouds, and
every eye shall see Him" (Rev. i. 7). In the
ecstasy of her new life the primitive Church looked
for the fulfilment of this great hope within the
Apostolic Age. "The coming of the Lord," she
said, "is at hand ; the Judge standeth before the
doors" (James v. 8, 9). "We that are alive
. . . are left unto the coming of the Lord"
(1 Thess. iv. 15). Her watchword was *Maran atha*
(1 Cor. xvi. 22)—"the Lord cometh," or perhaps
"the Lord come." "Amen, come, Lord Jesus,"
is her last word at the end of the New Testament
canon (Rev. xxii. 20). This expectation of an
imminent Return died with the first century, but
the assured hope of a Return lived on, and reflects
itself in all the Creeds of Christendom. The first
generation enshrined it in a series of Greek words,
which it borrowed from the common speech of the
time and consecrated to the service of the Faith.
The second coming of the Lord was called the
"Parousia" or Advent—a word used for the visit
of a Roman emperor or high official to the distant
parts of the Empire ; the "Epiphany" or Appearing ; the "Apocalypse" or Revelation of Jesus
Christ.* Christ, the King of Kings and Lord of
Lords, was coming to visit the earth. He would
manifest Himself to men in the full glory of the
Divine Manhood. He would drop the veil, which
since the Ascension has hidden Him from the eyes
of men, and stand revealed before the world.

To the question : For what purpose will He

* See Milligan on Thessalonians, p. 145 ff.

come ? the Apostolic Church had more than one
answer. He is coming to receive His people to
Himself, that where He is, in the Father's House,
they may be also (John xiv. 5). He is coming to
take to Himself His Bride, the Church, that she
may share His life with God (Eph. v. 27 ; Rev. xix.
7 f., xxi. 2 ff.). He will come to complete the work
of redemption by the resurrection of the body and
its rehabilitation after the fashion of His own
glorified manhood (Rom. viii. 23 ; 1 Cor. xv. 42 ff. ;
Phil. iii. 21). He will come to restore all things ;
to regenerate Nature, which is at length to be
delivered from the bondage of decay and the
frustration of its purpose (Matt. xix. 28 ; Acts iii.
21 ; Rom. viii. 19 ff. ; Rev. xxi. 5) ; to receive the
subjection of all things to Himself, and so to
complete His work as Mediator and bring in the
great consummation when God shall be all in all
(1 Cor. xv. 24–28). All these ends of our Lord's
Second Coming went to make up the fullness of the
hope which the first age connected with His Return.
The Creed, however, which limits itself to a few
essential articles of belief, passes them over, and
fixes attention upon a purpose of the Advent which
for the world in general is the most important and
interesting. "He shall come to judge the quick
and the dead."

When Jesus Christ was on earth He steadily
refused the office of judge. It was then no part
of His Messianic work. "Who made Me a judge
or a divider over you ? " (Luke xii. 13) was His
answer to one who invited Him to decide a question
of property. "Hath no man condemned thee ?
neither do I condemn thee," He is reported to have

said to an adulteress brought to Him for judgment
(John viii. 11)—not that He condoned adultery,
but because He had no authority to pronounce
sentence. To judge was not the purpose of the
First Coming. " God sent not the Son into the
world to judge the world, but that the world should
be saved through Him " (John iii. 17). " I judge
no man," Jesus said on another occasion, though
He could add : " If I judge, My judgment is true "
(John viii. 15 f.). And again : " If any man hear
My sayings and keep them not, I judge him not,
for I came not to judge the world, but to save the
world " (John xii. 47). Yet the Fourth Gospel,
which contains these strong disclaimers of judicial
authority, contains also our Lord's most distinct
claim to be the future Judge of men. " The
Father hath given all judgment unto the Son . . .
He gave Him authority to execute judgment,
because He is the Son of Man. . . . The hour
cometh in which all that are in the tombs shall hear
His voice and shall come forth ; they that have
done good, unto the resurrection of life, and they
that have done evil, unto the resurrection of
judgment " (John v. 22, 27 f.).

In one sense judgment is always going forward
in life and in history. The daily conduct of men
is a daily judgment, for it automatically divides
them by a moral grouping which goes to determine
their ultimate place in the Kingdom of God. It
forms character and habit, which will supply the
basis of final judgment. To this extent the First
Advent brought judgment, though its purpose
was not to judge but to save ; for it revealed the
true character of all who came into contact with

the Incarnate Life. "Thoughts out of many
hearts" were "revealed" (Luke ii. 35) by their
attitude towards Jesus Christ. "He that believeth
on Him," as St. John writes, "is not judged; he
that believeth not hath been judged already,
because he hath not believed on the name of the
only-begotten Son of God; and this is the judgment,
that the Light is come into the world, and men
loved the darkness rather than the Light" (John
iii. 18 ff.). Thus, notwithstanding His refusal of
judicial authority, our Lord could say: "For
judgment came I into this world" (John ix. 39);
and again, when the Crucifixion was at hand:
"Now is there a judgment of this world" (John xii.
31). Such a judicial process will continue to be a
result of the Incarnation and Atonement as long
as the world lasts and Christ is preached. Men
determine their own spiritual position by the
response which they make to the appeal of Christ
and His Church.

All this progressive judgment of man will find
its consummation at a future day. Of a "Day of
Judgment" the Gospel of St. Matthew speaks more
than once (Matt. xi. 15, 22, 24; xii. 36). The
phrase, which comes from the Greek Old Testament
(Isaiah xxxiv. 8), may stand for any time of trial
which sifts men or nations and reveals their moral
character; but in Christian use it becomes a title
for the time of the Second Advent (1 John iv. 17;
2 Peter ii. 9; iii. 7). This is also called the Great
Day, the Day of the Lord, the Day of Christ (Jude
6; 1 Peter iii. 10; Phil. ii. 16), in contrast with
"man's day" (1 Cor. iv. 3), *i.e.* the present
order, in which men and things are judged

according to merely human standards of right and wrong.

Imagination fails to paint the Great Assize of that day, even with the help of the symbolical descriptions which the New Testament supplies. Who can realise the gathering of all the generations of mankind before the glorified Christ, the nature of the scrutiny by which the secrets of all hearts shall be laid bare, the unerring justice of the verdict which will determine the result of all lives, the power which will make the sentence effective? The mind is staggered by the effort to grasp conditions to which our present life holds nothing analogous. In human courts of justice each case is heard separately, and the judgment is based on evidence which is elicited often with the greatest difficulty and which, when complete, may leave much to the summing up of the judge and the impression made by counsel on the minds of the jury. But before the Divine Tribunal all mankind will appear, and yet each individual will receive absolute justice. " I saw the dead, the great and the small, standing before the Throne, and books were opened; and they were judged every man according to their works " (Rev. xx. 12 f.). All the great men of history—kings and conquerors, statesmen and legislators, poets, philosophers, artists, men of letters, men of science—will be there, and with them the vast forgotten majority who " have no memorial," who to their fellow-men " are perished as though they had not been " (Ecclus. xliv. 9).

All are known to God, for " all live unto Him " (Luke xx. 38); all will receive equal attention; all will find the precise place for which their previous

lives have fitted them. None are too great to
stand before that Tribunal ; none too insignificant.
" Say not thou, I shall be hidden from the Lord,
and who shall remember me from on high ?   I shall
not be known among so many people ; for what is
my soul in a boundless creation ? " (Ecclus. xvi.
17).   Alive at the coming of the Lord, or already
for thousands of years among the dead, all human
beings will appear at the final reckoning and be
individually tried and sentenced.   Jesus Christ is
" ordained of God to be the Judge of quick and
dead " (Acts x. 42 ; 2 Tim. iv. 1).   " We shall not
all sleep " (*i.e.* die), " but we shall all be changed "
(1 Cor. xv. 51) ;   the living will undergo a transformation analogous to that which restores the
dead to life ;   so that, living or dead, we may all
stand together before the judgment seat of Christ.

One question calls for an answer at this point.
The New Testament everywhere represents the
Lord's Return as an object of joyful hope for the
Church.   Yet the prospect of standing before
the Supreme Judge is suggestive of awe or terror,
rather than of hope and joy.   Is it then to be
supposed that the faithful members of the Church
will be exempt from judgment ?   Will the Church
stand looking on while the world is being judged ?
These are passages in the New Testament, which,
taken by themselves, may seem to support this
view.   " He that believeth on the Son," St. John
writes, " is not being judged " (John iii. 18) ;   such
an one, our Lord Himself teaches, " cometh not
into judgment, but hath passed out of death into
life " (John v. 24).   St. Paul even speaks of the
members of Christ as His future assessors in

judgment (1 Cor. vi. 2 f.). But against the first impression which is created by words such as these we must set explicit statements that the judgment will be universal. The Great Master comes to reckon with all His servants, the good and faithful as well as the wicked and slothful; the sheep pass under the eye of the Shepherd as well as the goats. "We shall all stand" (St. Paul writes to the Roman Christians) "before the judgment seat of God; each one of us shall give account of himself to God" (Rom. xiv. 10 ff.). The Apostle does not hold himself exempt: "He that judgeth me is the Lord" (1 Cor. iv. 4); "we must all be made manifest before the judgment seat of Christ, that each one may receive the things done in the body" (2 Cor. v. 10). The faithful servant of Christ does not come into judgment in the sense that he is left in doubt of his acceptance; he comes to receive from the righteous Judge the crown of righteousness, which the Lord will give to those who have loved His appearing (2 Tim. iv. 8). Nevertheless he will be judged by the same unfailing truth and justice as the rest of mankind; there is no respect of persons with the Judge of all. There is enough of awfulness in the whole prospect to sober life, to induce watchfulness and diligence; but there is nothing in it to cloud the brightness of the hope with which the Church looks for the coming of her Lord.

Belief in a judgment after death is not peculiar to the Church. The doctrine that the actions of men will at some future time pass under review and receive an appropriate recompense, has been, in one form or another, widely held by pre-Christian

and non-Christian peoples. Both conscience and
reason assent to it. The Roman procurator, Felix,
whose violent and corrupt administration drew
upon him the censure of a heathen historian, "was
terrified" when his prisoner, Paul, reasoned of the
judgment to come (Acts xxiv. 25). His conscience,
hardened as it was, bore witness to the truth of the
Apostle's words. There is at times in the very
heathen, as the same Apostle suggests, something
like a rehearsal of the last assize, "their thoughts,
one with another, accusing or else excusing them"
(Rom. ii. 15) ; witnesses within them are already
giving evidence, as they will do with overwhelming
power when the great Day comes. Reason, too,
concurs with conscience, demanding that some
great review shall be made of human conduct.
Life, as we see it, is full of miscarriages of justice.
Vice is not always punished, nor is virtue always
rewarded while men are here. And looking back
over the pages of history we learn that it has always
been so ; there has never been hitherto any settling
of the long account, which nevertheless loudly calls
for settlement, if the world is under the government
of a righteous God. No Theist can resist the conclusion that a day of reckoning is yet to come ; the
unavenged crimes of thousands of years, the forgotten sins of millions of lives, await the coming
of a Supreme Judge. The world, or each life that
goes to make up the sum of human accountability,
must some day be judged in righteousness. When
St. Paul preached this doctrine on the Areopagus,
it excited, so far as we know, no opposition either
from Stoics or Epicureans ; they mocked when he
spoke of a resurrection, but the thought of a future

judgment excited no ridicule. There was in their deepest convictions something that responded to it, whatever their philosophical creeds might have led them to say. The principle of a Divine Judgment of the world and of individual men has always appealed to the reason as well as to the conscience of the majority of thoughtful men.*

The expectation of a future judgment, then, belongs to natural religion. But to this expectation Christianity gives definiteness and certainty ; it assigns a Day for the Judgment, it names the Judge. Jesus Christ, it says, is the Judge, and He will judge the world in the day of His Second Coming.

Men are to be judged by Man. This is an original feature in the Christian creed, and one which, if it excites interest and hope, also raises not a few difficulties. On the one hand, we feel the appropriateness of One Who is Himself " Son of Man " being entrusted with the work of judging His fellow-men. He will understand their nature ; He will be in sympathy with its sinless infirmities ; He will know the strength of its temptations, for He Himself has been tempted in all points like as we are. There is infinite kindness and love towards man shown in the delegation to Jesus Christ of all judgment, on the ground that He is Son of Man. On the other hand, the limitations of human nature seem to render the fulfilment of such a task by man impossible. How can man read the secrets of all hearts ? How can a human mind, however gigantic its intellectual strength, deal with the vast

* A useful summary of non-Christian opinion on this subject may be seen in Hastings' *Encyclopædia of Religion and Ethics*, s.v. *Eschatology* (v. p. 373 ff.).

mass of evidence, the infinite intricacies of life, the
complications arising from the influence of life on
life, of one generation on another; the immense
crowd of circumstances which, even in the case of a
single life, go to decide the measure of guilt or of
goodness; the maze of calculations necessary to
determine the exact award which each case requires?
The Incarnation alone can supply any approach to a
solution of this problem.   Even in the brief records
of the earthly life of Jesus Christ, we observe signs
that He possessed unique powers of reading
character at a glance; from the beginning of His
ministry He made it plain to those about Him that
" He knew all men, and needed not that any one
should bear witness concerning man, for He Himself knew what was in man " (John ii. 24 f).   Of the
powers of the glorified Christ, Who sits at the
right hand of God, and comes in the glory of the
Father, we can form no conception.*   But it may
well be believed that, when the world stands
before Him to be judged, He will need none to bear
witness concerning any of the countless lives with
which He has to deal.   " I am He," the Ascended
Christ has told us, " which searcheth the reins and
the heart " (Rev. ii. 23).   Behind the glorified
manhood, and working through it, is the personal
Word, Who, even more than the impersonal
revelation of God in Scripture and in conscience,
" pierces even to the dividing of soul and spirit,"
and is " quick " beyond all human experience
" to discern the thoughts and intents of the heart "
(Heb. iv. 12).

* The reader may refer to Bishop Weston's *The One Christ*, p. 287 ff.,
for some useful remarks on this point.

But, it may be said, God is Himself the One Judge of men. So the Old Testament repeatedly teaches (Gen. xviii. 25 ; Ps. l. 6 ; lxxv. 7 ; xciv. 2), and the Apostolic writers recognise this (Rom. xiv. 10 ff. ; probably, also, Rev. xx. 11). Judgment, universal and final, is a prerogative of God. There would seem to be no more elementary truth, and yet our Lord distinctly teaches that " the Father judgeth no man, but He hath given all judgment unto the Son " (John v. 22). " Who can forgive sins but one, even God ? " the scribes rightly asked ; and yet it is the Son of Man who has power on earth to forgive sins (Mark ii. 7, 10). So also to the Son of Man is committed the Divine prerogative of judgment. Since the Incarnation this world is in the hands of a Mediator, and to Him all authority is given so long as the period of mediation lasts. The Judgment is the last act in this devolution of Divine prerogatives to the Incarnate Son ; with it the Kingdom of the Mediator ceases, merged in the eternal reign of God. It is God Who will judge the secrets of men, but He will judge them by Jesus Christ (Rom. ii. 16).

A few words must be added on the sentences which the Judge will pronounce, for these, too, have been revealed to us, although they are not named in the Creed. The Judge Himself ends His description of the judgment scene with the appalling words, " These " (the condemned) " shall go away into eternal punishment, but the righteous into eternal life." This is not the place to consider the meaning of " eternal " in such a connection, or of " punishment " and " life " ; a discussion of these words would lead us too far afield, and carry us into regions of thought which the human mind, as it is at present constituted, cannot explore. But there is one feature which is common to all the New Testament descriptions of the future judgment, and which challenges our attention. It is the sharp dividing line which is to be drawn by the Judge, on one side of which, or on the other, all human beings must ultimately find themselves. In life, as we know it, there is no such clearly marked line between good and evil, and no tests which we can apply would place one part of mankind on the right hand, and the rest on the left. Most living men seem to us to be on the border, or on neutral ground, neither wholly good nor wholly bad, or fluctuating from day to day between the two opposite sides. Even when a life is ended, and we read a careful review of it in a published memoir or in history, we often hesitate to pronounce judgment of complete condemnation or complete approval. But the Supreme Judge, as it appears, will not hesitate, will find none to whom justice and truth can assign an intermediate place between the saved and the lost. He possesses a knowledge of the secrets of the heart which is denied to us ; tests of character will be at His disposal which we cannot apply. Moreover, the fluctuations of motive and purpose which exist here will have ceased ; before the end each man will have definitely taken his side, and the Judge will but confirm the sentence which the soul has, in fact, passed upon itself.

Other difficulties, admitting only of a partial solution, may occur to the mind as it contemplates the Christian doctrine of the judgment to come. But intellectual perplexities will not disturb the

K

faith of the thoughtful Christian; he recognises them, but they leave his belief unshaken. It would surprise him if an event so remote from all present experience presented no difficulties but such as the limited powers of man's understanding were able to solve. He does not profess to understand all the contents of his Creed, which, resting on a basis of historical facts, runs up into mysteries which are as yet unexplained. He waits for the future to reveal many things which for the present he is content to believe.

Meanwhile, the practical effect of belief in Jesus Christ as Judge is not weakened by the impossibility of realising the scene, or analysing the contents of our faith. Faith in the return of our Lord as the Judge of quick and dead changes the whole tenor of the present life. It lifts up common work and intercourse into the presence of Christ.* It ennobles all the service of the world by inspiring it with the hope of the Master's approval; it encourages vigilance, thoroughness, faithfulness. For believers the Tribunal of Christ stands at the end of all their ways, and imparts to life a solemn joy which at once chastens and brightens their years on earth. "We make it our aim whether at home or absent," whether we shall be found among the dead or the living when He comes, "to be well-pleasing unto Him," our Saviour and our Judge. We seek to "abide in Him, that, if He shall be manifested, we may have boldness, and not be ashamed before Him at His coming" (2 Cor. v. 9; 1 John ii. 28).

* Christians "talk as men who know that the Lord hears them" (Tertullian, *Apology*, ch. 39).

IX

THE HOLY SPIRIT

" I believe in the Holy Ghost."

BELIEF in the Holy Ghost dominates the third great paragraph of the Christian Creed; on it depend all the Articles which assert belief in the Church and the forgiveness of sins and immortality; it is clearly of fundamental importance for Christian faith. If we would understand it aright there are three points with which we must deal: (1) How did belief in the Holy Spirit arise? (2) How did it develop? (3) What does it mean?

I.—HOW DID BELIEF IN THE HOLY SPIRIT ARISE?

The Christian Church has always based its theology on facts, and there are certain definite, historical facts at the basis of its belief in the Holy Spirit. What are they?

They are facts in the actual experience of the Apostles of our Lord and of other primitive Christians, facts which in the last resort can only be accounted for by the emergence of a new spiritual power at work in the lives of men, the power which they called " The Holy Spirit."

To see what these facts are we must concentrate

our attention first on the problem presented by those seven weeks which are and must remain the most momentous in the history of mankind, the seven weeks which elapsed between that Passover on the eve of which Jesus was crucified for claiming to be the Messiah, and that Pentecost on the morning of which St. Peter preached the first Christian sermon.

The Feast of Passover begins with the disciples hiding in terror of their lives, disillusioned, hopeless, faithless: their Master executed for blasphemy, dead and buried : He who should have redeemed Israel overwhelmed with failure and disgrace, forsaken and rejected, as it seemed, alike by man and by God. The Feast of Pentecost finds those same disciples publicly repeating that very claim that Jesus was the Messiah, which, when He Himself had made it, had caused His death. It was St. Peter, whose cowardice had denied all knowledge of Jesus when He was on trial, who now proclaimed, " Let all the house of Israel know assuredly that God hath made this same Jesus whom ye crucified both Lord and Christ." At the Passover all was darkness and despair ; at Pentecost all was confidence and light.

How are we to account for this amazing contrast ? The Apostles' conviction that the crucified Jesus was the exalted Messiah remains a psychological enigma, inexplicable, unless we can assume as its cause an objective, historical fact, as objective and historical as the Crucifixion itself, a fact which persuaded His disciples that Jesus was alive after His death. Such a fact was the Resurrection, of which tradition assures us they became aware on the morning next but one after His burial.

But why, if they knew of the Resurrection so soon, did the Apostles wait seven weeks before proclaiming it to the world ? If we study the accounts of that interval which have come down to us, we discover good reasons for the delay : not only did it take time to convince the disciples of Jesus' Resurrection, but, more important still, when they were convinced of it they were also convinced that they were not yet adequately fitted to proclaim it. They must wait till they were endued with " power from on high " ; so they learnt from their experience of the Risen Christ Himself.

At length the Resurrection Appearances culminated in one which impressed them with the sense of its finality, and of the completeness of their Master's triumph—the Appearance known to Church tradition as the Ascension. Convinced that they were entrusted with the duty of proclaiming Him as Lord and Saviour, about a hundred and twenty disciples gathered in Jerusalem under the leadership of the Apostles ; there they waited for their opportunity and the power to use it.

With the Feast of Pentecost the opportunity arrived ; it was now or never ; and with the opportunity came the expected power : as a rushing mighty wind, as a fire that blazed from heaven, it was upon them ; it lit up their minds to see the real meaning of all that Jesus had taught and done, the true significance of His sufferings and His triumph ; it compelled them to proclaim with burning eloquence all that they had learnt of the mighty works of God; and from that day onwards it dominated their lives and actions.

God had sent into their hearts through Jesus Christ a Power not of this world: only such a power could achieve what history assures us was achieved by those early Christians. By its compelling influence they found themselves welded together into a religious and social community, a fellowship of faith and hope and love, the true Israel, the Church of the living God. Enabled to become daily more and more like Jesus, they developed an ever fuller comprehension of His unique significance; and so they went about carrying on the work and teaching which He had begun on earth, certain that He was with them and energising in them. They healed the sick in mind and body, they convinced Jewish and Pagan consciences of sin and its forgiveness, they created a new morality, and established a new hope; life and immortality were brought to light. And then, as need arose, they were inspired to write those books of the New Testament, in which their wonderful experience of God at work in them remains enshrined, the norm and standard of Christian faith and practice for all time.

The Power which enabled them to do all this they called the Holy Spirit. For the first Christians the Holy Spirit signified no mere theological concept, but a potent actuality of everyday experience, alive and active, with all the force and vitality of a living person. Just as they could no longer think of God except as they now knew Him revealed as the Father of our Lord Jesus Christ, so they could no longer think of the Son of God except as they now knew Him in and through the working of the Holy Spirit. Father, Son and Holy Spirit were inseparable in their thoughts of God.

II.—THE DEVELOPMENT OF THE DOCTRINE OF THE SPIRIT

The word which we translate as " Spirit " had already had a long history. First it had been used by the primitive Hebrews for the breath of man, and the wind of heaven, both of them mysterious forces of life and motion beyond human control; and then it was used to describe such instances of strength and skill, of wisdom and sanctity, as seemed so far beyond the normal scope of human capacities as to be explicable only as the work of some Divine agency; in the words and deeds of men so remarkably endowed the Jews believed they saw the breath—that is, the actual vital force —of God Himself, energising in and through men. The later Jewish Church recognised in the inspiration of the great prophets the highest manifestation of the Spirit's working yet seen, but the prophets themselves pointed forward to a yet fuller outpouring of His power; when the Messiah came, not only would He Himself be supremely endowed with the Spirit, but as a result of His coming His people one and all would experience such an outpouring of His influence as had never before been known.

It was this great expectation which the Apostles of Jesus declared had been at length fulfilled. It was well known, they said, that " God had anointed Jesus of Nazareth with the Holy Ghost and with power "; and the early accounts of our Lord's earthly ministry give us a vivid picture of one in whom the Spirit moved mightily; at His baptism He had a vision of the Spirit descending upon Him; immediately afterwards the Spirit " drives " Him into the wilderness to face the great temptation; " in the power of the Spirit " He begins to preach; by the same power He claims to cast out devils; and in a moment of sublime exaltation He is described as " rejoicing in the Holy Spirit." Just before His death He tells His disciples that when they, like their Master before them, find themselves confronted by the authorities of a hostile world, they will discover that this same Holy Spirit they see working in His ministry is working also in theirs: " it is not ye that speak, but the Holy Spirit."

And the Acts of the Apostles is the record of how this promise came true: it begins with the Pentecostal outpouring of the Spirit, to which the Apostles point as clear and immediate proof of the Messiahship of Jesus; and throughout the rest of the book the Holy Spirit dominates the story. Not only the characters and exploits of individual believers, but the corporate acts and decisions of the Church are controlled by His inspiration; the leading motive of the narrative is nothing else than this: that what Jesus had begun to do and teach in His earthly ministry He now, in His heavenly exaltation, continues and develops through His disciples by the agency of the Holy Spirit. The Acts has well been called " The Gospel of the Holy Spirit."

The letters of St. Paul give us an even more vivid picture of the direct action of the Spirit in early Christian experience. Like a number of his fellow Christians then and since at times of great religious crisis and "revival," he found himself possessed of certain abnormal psychical capacities, such as the faculty for " seeing visions " and "speaking with tongues." But, whereas his converts were all too ready to value most highly those "spiritual gifts," which seemed to them most thrilling and inexplicable, he valued most highly those which contributed most to the building of the Christian community, and chief among them he set faith and hope and love.

The presence of the Spirit in men's hearts, he teaches, sets them free ; no longer enslaved by the letter of the law, they find themselves capable of leading an entirely new kind of life, the dominant characteristics of which are "love, joy, peace, long-suffering, kindness, goodness, faithfulness, meekness, self-control." These are none other than the characteristics of the perfect humanity of Christ, and it is precisely in this constant ability of believing Christians to lead a Christ-like life that St. Paul sees the supreme function of God's Spirit operating in men. The Spirit enables men, here and now, to share in the heavenly life of the risen Christ, setting them free from the power of sin and death, and ensuring them an immortality of Christlikeness.

The Fourth Gospel interprets our Lord's life and teaching, as given in the earlier records, in the light of half a century's experience of Christianity. For St. John, no less than the earlier New Testament writers, the Holy Spirit is not an abstract idea, but a living force, the very life-breath of the ever-living Christ, breathed into His disciples as the climax of His redemptive work. So profoundly impressed is this Evangelist with the way in which the Spirit's operation in the Christian Church surpasses all that has ever been before, that, speaking of the days of our Lord's earthly ministry, he actually says, "The Spirit was not yet." This does not imply that God's Spirit has not always been at work among men, but that the Incarnation heralds a new stage of spiritual manifestation, in the splendour of which all that has preceded it fades into insignificance. For in the Coming of the Spirit the Son Himself returns to dwell as an inward power in men's lives, and with the Son the Father also; it follows that to have the Spirit means to have fellowship with the Father and the Son, that is, to be drawn into the very life of the Eternal God. And so the Spirit is called the "Paraclete," or "Comforter," a title which signifies that He comes to our aid, to be our counsel and defence, a Divine adviser and strengthener, who, now that the Son's visible presence is withdrawn, takes His place. Essentially the Spirit of Truth and Reality, He opens men's eyes to see the Divine Reality as it has been revealed in the Son. By bringing to their remembrance what the Son had taught while on earth, and by unfolding its innermost meaning, He explains, re-interprets, and applies to the ever-changing needs and conditions of the growing Church the teaching of the historical Jesus. He will abide with the disciples for ever, not merely during the age of the Apostles, in order to declare to them " things as they are coming."

The men who wrote such things about the

Spirit did so because they knew them to be true. Their interest was practical rather than theoretical : they were concerned not so much to construct a complete and scientific system of Christian theology as to describe and impart to others an intense and vivid personal experience of an astonishing kind. The New Testament brings us into touch with men who had known a unique Personality ; they were convinced that the one thing that supremely mattered was that the character of Jesus Christ, His thoughts about God and man, and sin and happiness, His purity, His love, His self-sacrifice, should be reproduced in as many human beings as possible, that the richness of His amazing vitality should pass into and transform their lives. They knew that this was no idle dream, but a glorious possibility, because it was happening in themselves ; and the Divine Power that was bringing it about they worshipped and glorified as the Holy Spirit, the Lord, the Life-giver.

The doctrine of the Holy Spirit did not particularly occupy the attention of the Church's theologians till His Deity was challenged by the Arians in the fourth century. As that great controversy developed it became clear that belief in the Spirit was vitally affected by belief in the Son : the Arians who denied that Jesus Christ was " very God of very God, of one substance with the Father," began to assert that the Holy Spirit was little more than the influence of Christ's example, a gift to men, a thing created, in no sense an essential reality in the eternal life of God Himself. Athanasius and those who thought with him answered in effect that if Christ, the Son of God, be indeed of the very substance of the Godhead, no less Divine than the Father Himself, the Holy Spirit, through whose agency the Divine Son is conveyed into the lives and hearts of the faithful, cannot be less Divine than He Whom He conveys, and is therefore also of the very substance of the Godhead : Father, Son and Spirit, one God. They had on their side not only logic, but the sense of Scripture and Church tradition ; above all, the general religious experience of Christendom supported them and not their opponents. Consequently when, at the Second General Council at Constantinople, the Church finally rejected Arianism, and reaffirmed the Nicene Creed, it also sanctioned a second form of Creed, containing these words about the Holy Ghost : " And I believe in the Holy Ghost, the Lord and Giver of life, Who proceedeth from the Father, Who with the Father and the Son together is worshipped and glorified, Who spake by the prophets."

It is a well-known fact that one of the reasons why Western Christendom under the Popes finally broke off from the Orthodox Churches of the East in 1054 was the insertion into this Creed of the word "*Filioque*" (="and from the Son ") after the words "Who proceedeth from the Father." The Easterns regard this as an unauthorised tampering with an inviolable formula ; the actual theological point in dispute was a matter of terms rather than of doctrine ; charity and good will would have discovered that both sides were in essential agreement, had not ecclesiastical rivalry driven out charity and good will. Pope and Patriarch really excommunicated each other because they were rivals for the Sovereignty of Christendom : there is a tragic fitness in the fact that as a cloak for their ambitions they used a dispute about the nature of the Spirit of Love and Unity.

III.—WHAT DOES BELIEF IN THE HOLY SPIRIT MEAN ?

We have traced in bare outline the course of experience and of thought about experience which has led the Christian Church to include belief in the Holy Spirit among the fundamental articles of its Creed. We have seen that this belief originated in certain concrete, historical occurrences, which demanded an explanation. The doctrine of the Holy Spirit was founded on fact ; it was not the outcome of abstract theological speculation. Yet for the majority of Christians to-day it seems to be little better than an abstruse and unintelligible formula, far removed from the practical necessities of everyday life. If it is to become for us of the twentieth century what it certainly was for the Christians of the early Church—a vital factor dominating characters and actions—it can only be if we discover in our doctrine of the Holy Spirit truths which are of essential value for our own thought and life. Do the words, " I believe in the Holy Ghost " enshrine for us any such essential truths ? I believe they do.

Let us take that unpromising word " proceeding," that technical term describing the function of the Holy Spirit about which Greek and Latin theologians quarrelled so disastrously in the eleventh century. Our first feeling about it is that it is a figment of antiquated theology which the Church had better forget ; yet, as a matter of fact, " proceeding " sums up in one word just what, from first to last, the Bible tells us about the Holy Spirit's activity. Throughout the Old and New Testaments the Spirit is presented to our thought as a Divine Power issuing out of God, by which the Divine Life operates beyond itself, if we may be forgiven such a crudely spatial expression. In the Universe He has created, and, above all, in the lives of men, God Himself is at work, in and through His Spirit : that is the basal truth safeguarded by the doctrine of the " Procession " of the Spirit ; and it is obviously of very great importance both for Christian thought and Christian practice.

First and foremost, it secures for Christian thought an adequate conception of the Nature of God, both as He is in Himself and as He is in relation to the world.

(a) *God as He is in Himself.*—If we believe that the Holy Spirit is an essential reality in the Eternal Being of God, we are at once assured that the nature of the Divine Life is not static but dynamic ; in other words, that God is a living God—not an idea, but a force. His is no motionless eternity of perfection, but an overflowing vitality, an inexhaustible fecundity, the everlasting well-spring of all existence. Out of the depths of the Divine Nature there flows unceasingly an infinitude of love and truth and beauty which constitutes the transcendent happiness of God as He is in Himself, the Supreme and Perfect Being.

(b) *God in His Relation to the World.*—And

because He is a living God He does not keep Himself to Himself. His life is an overflowing life, and creation is the vessel into which it overflows. He has brought into existence this finite world of space and time that it may share His bliss; for all His ineffable transcendence we cannot think of Him simply as a distant and external First Cause of the Universe; always there is proceeding from Him that life force which we call His Spirit, to operate in the vast evolving processes of the world, and to give imperishable value to all that is true and good and beautiful in this transitory sphere of space and time.

Thus Christianity maintains the truth of God's immanence in the world as well as of His transcendence above it; it recognises the operation of the ever-proceeding Spirit in all the wonders of Nature, and in every work of art and every discovery of knowledge which enriches civilisation and enlarges human life.

But, above all, it venerates, as the highest operation of the Spirit, that which He is perpetually doing in the sphere of Christianity itself, as He " sanctifieth the elect people of God," reproducing Christ in Christians. Were it not for this Power of the Spirit Christianity would be the despair instead of the hope of men; for in the Person of Jesus Christ we should see revealed a perfection at once human and divine, which nevertheless remained for ever unattainable by weak and sinful humanity. Like men who, shipwrecked in a tempestuous sea, catch sight of the sunlit beauties of a land which their failing strength can never reach, so we, beholding from our powerlessness the glory of God reflected in the face of Jesus Christ, would know that not for us was that bright life of Heaven, were it not that " the Spirit helpeth our infirmities," and can transform us into Christlikeness, from glory to glory. So it is in this specifically Christian experience of the Spirit's power as " He proceedeth from the Father through the Son," that men realise His influence in the world at its highest.

In its practical aspect the doctrine of the Procession of the Spirit implies this : that the Religion of the Spirit can never stand still ; like the Spirit Himself it must ever be going forth, expanding, progressing. Wherever we find stagnation and reaction, there the Spirit of Life is being resisted and quenched ; in the life both of the individual and of the Church utter selfishness and self-satisfaction may shut out the Wind of Heaven.

It follows that Christianity must be from its very nature (a) a growing and progessive movement, and (b) a movement embodied in and energising through a society.

(a) Both as a system of thought and as a system of practical conduct a really spiritual Christianity will be always growing and expanding ; Christians can never at any given moment know all that is to be known of God's truth, as it stands revealed yet hidden in Christ ; the ever-moving stream of history brings Christianity perpetually up against new crises, new problems, new discoveries, new forces, philosophical, scientific, political ; it is the function of the Holy Spirit to impart to Christ's disciples the mind of Christ, and thus to enable them to bring to bear upon the data of our increasing experience Christ's ideals, Christ's principles, Christ's methods, so that Christians in all.places and in all ages may deal with the circumstances in which they find themselves as Jesus Himself would deal with them, were He still incarnate here on earth. The Christian Church, like the Christ Himself, should increase in wisdom as it increases in stature; it should always be learning, that it may always be teaching; it should shirk no difficulty, it should welcome all new light, proving all things, holding fast to that which is good. The timidity and slackness that shrink from facing the re-statements and re-adjustments of creed and organisation that advancing knowledge and changing conditions necessitate are unworthy of those who profess a belief in the Holy Spirit; a faith which shirks criticism and self-criticism is no gift of His.

(b) Christianity, as the religion of "the Spirit which proceedeth," is in its very nature a social religion. We cannot as individual believers keep the Spirit for ourselves; if we will not share Him with others, if He fails to find a way by which He can proceed through our lives into yet other lives, He leaves us. He is the Spirit of Fellowship, of Unity, of Love; and Love can never live in isolation whether in God or in man; Love must be poured forth on others or it ceases to be Love; hence it is that the Spirit of God, Who is Love, carries on the life and work of Christ in humanity not through mere individuals as such, but through individuals who are members of a society. The Christian Society, the Holy Catholic Church, came into existence to be the ideal sphere of the Spirit's

L

operation, created not by man but by the Spirit; in it faith and hope and love are embodied and organised. Only in proportion as its members subordinate their individual interests to its corporate welfare, and contribute to its common life the gifts which the Spirit gives to each, will they themselves be enriched and strengthened, until they all grow up together into that perfect manhood which the Incarnation of the Son of God has made possible for all.

And the Christian Society itself, like the Christian individual, cannot keep the life of the Spirit within it to itself without being false to the very principle of its existence; unless the Church is doing its utmost to impart its own inspiration to the rest of humanity as yet outside the Church, its own inspiration flags and dies. From its very nature, as the Spirit-bearing Body, the Christian Church must be a missionary church or cease to be itself.

But because the Spirit of Selfishness, which is the age-long enemy of the Spirit of Love, is not yet killed, Christendom, instead of being one strong united worldwide Commonwealth of Christ, is a welter of self-seeking sects. Everywhere the action of the Spirit is being thwarted by our divisions, and the disunion of Christendom is one chief reason why Christian experience of the Power of the Holy Spirit is to-day so dim and vague.

Christians must face the facts and discern the signs of the times. At the present moment there are other groups and societies of men where fellowship and social co-operation flourish more than they do in the Christian Church; it is a fact that to-day a man may often learn, through membership of a college, or a regiment, or a labour organisation, more of the force and the inspiration which come into a life as the result of self-devotion to the common good, than most men ever learn through membership in the Christian Body. The Spirit of Truth and Love and Power is " a wind which bloweth where it listeth," and for some of God's good purposes for men that Spirit is just now more active and effectual outside the Christian society than within it.

To recognise this fact is not dishonourable to Christians, but to acquiesce in it is disgrace. How can the Church best set about remedying this disastrous state of things ? Only by setting itself once more to discover and then to live by the " truth as it is in Jesus." But if we are to hope to get at that truth we must employ means and methods which we can believe are those of the Holy Spirit of Truth Himself. Is not the shattered unity of Christendom itself a proof that Christians in the past have not used Christian methods for arriving at that truth which should unite and not divide them ? And, now that Christendom is thus divided, is it not clear that not one of its sections can rightly claim to know the whole of Christian truth so long as it is content to remain in complete isolation from the rest ? Yet the continued existence of so many and so varied Christian societies in spite of their separation from each other is in itself a sign that each of them inherits some valuable and abiding truth of doctrine or of discipline, which it has cultivated but others have ignored ; clearly, then, we must abandon those mad methods of controversy which have made "odium theologicum" proverbially the bitterest of all hatreds, and learn, though still divided, to co-operate as best we can. And already we are learning : we are learning to respect the convictions of others as we rightly respect our own ; we are learning to pray together, to study together, and to act together, in spite of our great differences ; we are learning that in religion affirmation is more fruitful than negation, and that truth is more often comprehensive than exclusive. And just in those movements among Christians where all this is being learnt are men experiencing once more the living inspiration of a Power not theirs but God's. The Holy Spirit is still with us, and if we will but let Him He will yet guide us into all the truth.

And as the Spirit teaches us we must act upon what He teaches ; the Church must not shrink from experiments and adventures, it must be prepared to "live dangerously," as it did in the great days of old. Our Saviour promised the Spirit's divine assistance to disciples who were ready, for His Name's sake, to bear their witness in face of persecutions ; and we, too, must have the courage of our convictions, cost what it may, if we are to expect the Spirit to make of us Christians of to-day what He made of those first disciples.

We, like them, are men on whom the "ends of the ages are come." An old world is in its death agony, a new world is struggling to its birth ; and as then out of terror and darkness the Eternal Christ arose and gave His Spirit to His own, so, too, to us will He vouchsafe another Pentecost, and renew the face of the earth.

X

THE HOLY TRINITY

IT is indeed no ungrateful task to write for the National Mission a paper on the doctrine of the Trinity. The mind of the Christian Englishman has, like every other mind, its own tendencies to misbelief, but it has no such tendency here. Heresy as to the doctrine of the Trinity belongs to the East rather than to the West, and the Englishman is a Western of the Westerns. He may misunderstand the mind of the Church, and so suppose himself to differ from it, but there is no real severance ; the Church thinks as he thinks and feels as he feels. If at times she speaks as he does not speak, that is only because she has had dangers against which to guard of which the Christian Englishman is unaware. Let him but understand the Church, and he will approve her attitude as the Church approves his

What is the mind of the Christian Englishman as he thinks of God ? Most profoundly does he believe in Father, Son, and Holy Spirit. Jesus is his Saviour, the Lord and Master of his life, and he longs to drink deep of His Spirit. But he desires a simple and, above all, a practical religion, and he has little interest in religious speculation. For his own part, he does not expect to understand the mystery of the Godhead. The theologians of the Church may see farther than he does, but before such a mystery we must all be as little children. Religion, he is sure, should be a thing of the heart and of the life rather than of the head; it is what we are and do that matters. His dislike of the Athanasian Creed is largely rooted in intellectual humility. He does not think that he knows better than the Church, or desire to correct her teachings; but he does not see how anybody can really know as much about God as the Church there seems to him to claim to know. He wishes by the Spirit to serve God and follow his Master Christ, and the Athanasian Creed seems to hinder rather than to help him. Does the Church blame him for adopting this attitude? Rather she meets him at almost every point with enthusiastic agreement. But there is just one thing which the Christian Englishman has overlooked. The members of the Church have not all taken so modest a view of their powers as the Englishman. Many in the past have not been at all willing to take mysteries patiently, and, in trying to clear them up, they have really denied or explained away the facts upon which the Christian life depends. "Because this Divine mystery," says Richard Hooker, "is more true than plain, divers, having framed the same to their own conceits and fancies, are found in their expositions thereof more plain than true." Thus the Church has been obliged in the interests of the Christian life to insist upon the facts, and to repudiate these denials and explanations in language as explicit as she could find. Her best teachers deplored the necessity, and said plainly that they deplored it ; * it was torture to them to treat the truths revealed in God's dealings with us as if they were propositions in Euclid, and to define where they only wished to adore. But if, when the Church spoke in her own reverent and cautious way, men insisted that she meant what she did not mean, and could not mean without forfeiting the foundations of her life, what would the Englishman himself have her do ? The whole purpose of the Church is to insist upon facts ; she demands of us, as we shall presently see, the acceptance of no theories which go beyond them.

How, let us ask, can we know God ? Can our little minds understand all the mystery of His nature ? Obviously not. Indeed, there is nothing that we can know in its entirety except the conceptions of our own minds. Take, for example, a straight line, as Euclid defines it. The straight line is simply a mental conception—there are no straight lines in nature—and therefore it presents no difficulty. Define it as Euclid defines it, and you can know about it all that there is to be known. But contrast with the straight line the very smallest beetle. The beetle is a humble portion of reality ; the beetle is actually there ; and thus we might spend a lifetime in the study of the beetle,

* Cf. the language of St. Hilary, *De Trinitate,* II. 2 (quoted by Tyrrell, *Through Scylla and Charybdis,* p. 354, note). " We are forced through the fault of heretics and blasphemers to do that which is unlawful, to climb inaccessible heights, to speak what cannot be uttered, to encroach upon what is forbidden. And whereas we should be content to find out by simple faith what we have to do—namely, to adore the Father and venerate with Him the Son, to abound in the Holy Ghost—we are compelled to stretch the littleness of our discourse to the compass of matters unspeakable, and are driven to wrong-doing through the wrong-doing of others : so that what should be treasured in the devout soul is now committed to all the dangers of human language."

and know him but imperfectly at the end of it. Now if this be so with all reality, how imperfect must be our knowledge of God, the highest reality of all ! If the world is as complex and as wonderful as we find it, what should we expect that God would be found to be ? That He is a Trinity in Unity no doubt appears to higher intelligences than ours a merely elementary truth about Him. The nature of God would indeed be simple if that were all that there were to be known. Thus all that we can know of God is just what He reveals to us, and not even His Divine skill can reveal to us more than our little minds are able to receive. That is not to say that we can know nothing of God, or that our knowledge of Him is not real knowledge as far as it goes. To say that would be not merely to exhibit a distrust of our faculties of knowledge, which is quite irrational, but also to deny to God Himself the power of self-revelation.* St. Paul says that we are made to seek God, if haply we may feel after Him, and find Him. Certainly God can reveal Himself, if He desires to do so, and the religious experience of men assures us that He has so desired. We do find God—" not His semblance, but Himself " ; the religious instinct would not have survived, had it not been in contact with reality. But—and this is the great point to be observed—we must depend upon facts for our knowledge of God from first to

---

* Of course, all knowledge is relative to our human faculties ; the eye can only see what it brings with it the power of seeing. But this no more makes our knowledge of God unreliable than it makes our knowledge of the world unreliable. Trust in our faculties is as necessary to physical science as to theology.

last, and we cannot know in advance what will be revealed. It is with our knowledge of God just as it is with our knowledge of the world about us ; facts, and not abstract reasoning, must be our guide. In the Middle Ages the minds of men were by no means destitute of ideas about the world in which we live, but those ideas were largely erroneous, and therefore misleading, because they had little except speculation upon which to rest. Nowadays we are humbler. The man of science to-day makes considerable use of speculation and hypothesis, but it is facts upon which he mainly relies ; carefully and laboriously he investigates facts, and tests his hypotheses by them. That does not render his conclusions simpler than those of the Middle Ages—very far from it ; but it does render them immeasurably truer. So it is with our knowledge of God. If it is to be reliable, it must rest upon facts. A true knowledge of God is very unlikely to give us a simple view of Him ; the conception of the Unitarian is a great deal too simple to be true. But truth is of far more practical importance than simplicity can ever be, and it is facts which must lead us to it.

How, then, has the Christian view of God been actually reached ? By a frank reliance upon the facts of human history and experience. The Hebrews, unlike the Greeks, had no gifts for philosophy. They do not seem in any conscious way even to have reasoned from the world to the existence of God.* Their interest in God was

---

* The witness of the world to God is a witness drawn from experience. But Ps. xix. 1–6 and similar passages are probably not inconsistent with the view expressed above. They are not statements of the

almost entirely practical; they were not concerned with the question what God might be in His own interior life. But of this they were certain. Their God had revealed Himself to them in the facts of their history and experience, and there was no doubt as to what the revelation had been. At first they had thought of Him much as other Semitic peoples thought of the " gods many, and lords many," in whom they believed, but He Himself convinced them that He was far other than they. He had a purpose—so the Hebrews found— and in the working out of His purpose there was nothing which could say Him nay. He dealt with nations and with men as only their Maker and Lord could deal with them. He had brought His people Israel out of Egypt with a mighty Hand and a stretched-out Arm; He had planted them in their own land; all the gods of the heathen had been as nothing before Him. He had chosen Israel for His own people, and made a covenant with them. He had given them His holy law, and shown Himself able to vindicate it when they set it aside. Marvellously gracious He was, marvellously long-suffering, but He was strict none the less; He would by no means clear the guilty, and somehow the consequences of sin did not die with those who committed it. So, by the witness of facts, the Hebrews came to know the Name * of Yahveh

' cosmological ' and " teleological " arguments for God's existence. The Hebrews seem to have reached their belief that God was the Creator and Lord of the world by their own national experience, and to have employed the world as a witness to Him after they had done so.

* " The Name of Yahveh " in Holy Scripture is ever in the closest connection with Yahveh Himself. It is the expression of His character and attributes. Where God's Name is, He is. " The Name of Yahveh is a strong tower," because it expresses all that He has shown Himself

their God—" Yahveh, Yahveh, a God full of
compassion and gracious, slow to anger, and
plenteous in mercy and truth ; keeping mercy for
thousands, forgiving iniquity and transgression
and sin, and that will by no means clear the guilty ;
visiting the iniquity of the fathers upon the children,
upon the third and upon the fourth generation."
Beautiful stories had come down to them of
Yahveh's proclamation of His Name, but the great
proclamation was not in word, but in fact. The
Hebrews did not believe that God was Almighty,
or All-wise, or All-holy, or All-gracious because
their philosophers had proved that He must be so,
or even mainly because their seers had declared
that He was so ; they believed it because their
whole national experience had established the truth
upon the rock of fact.

But what of Yahveh's inner nature ? Was He
manifold, as well as one ? This the Hebrews were
far too exclusively practical to consider. He was
One in the sense that there was none other than He,
all the gods of the heathen being but vanity ; but
further than this they hardly went. They did
not indeed think of Him as a bare and barren unity.
Though the Holy One of Israel was raised immeasurably above the world and the turmoil of
human life, He had revealed Himself within them
both. His Divine Wisdom, though brought forth
before the world, joyously realised itself before Him
in the world itself.* The stories, which had come

---

to be to us. Similarly, such names as Peter and Boanerges are the
expression of the character of those who bear them—of what they are
to the Lord and to their brethren.

* Prov. viii. 22–31 and similar descriptions of the Divine Wisdom in
the Apocrypha lie behind John i. 1–3, Col. i. 15–17, and Heb. i. 1–3.

down from the past, spoke frequently of a mysterious angel of Yahveh, in whom was Yahveh's Name, Their heroes, their seers, even their craftsmen were what they were because the Spirit of Yahveh was within them. But such facts did not stir them to theological speculation as they might have stirred the Greeks; they took the facts as they found them, and neither philosophised about them nor explained them away. Very English all this was ; no nation can in this understand the Hebrews better than we can ourselves.

Thus far for the Old Testament. And then into the world of experience Jesus of Nazareth came, and in Him their God drew nearer to them than ever He had drawn before. Of Him it was true far more wonderfully than of any Angel of the Lord in bygone days, that God's Name was in Him. He was " the wisdom of God and the power of God," " the effulgence of His glory and the very image of His substance "—not in theory, but in fact. There, plainly manifested in Him and through Him, were the very redeeming power, the very holiness, the very wisdom and authority, the very patience and long-suffering of God Himself. And not only had He this Name ; He spoke and bore Himself as One Who had it. His language was seldom, if ever, theological language. He spoke of the Father, and of His own relation to the Father, out of the heart of His own spiritual experience. Distinct from the Father He certainly was, in every act and word subordinate to Him. His whole life and bearing were a proclamation that the Father was greater than He. But His followers found in Him God Himself ; He spoke with an authority which God alone could exercise; He claimed a devotion which to God alone could rightly be given; He promised to do, and did, a work beyond all human power; He said that wherever two or three were gathered in His Name He would be in the midst of them.* So it was with the Spirit, which He promised. God's Name was in Him too. He too was found, in the experience of the Church, to possess the redeeming power, the holiness, the wisdom, the authority, the patience of God Himself. As the Son had been to the Father, so the Spirit proved to be to the Son, distinct from Him in some sense, and yet mysteriously one with Him. He witnessed to the Son, glorified the Son in the minds of men, took of what was the Lord's and manifested it, and yet at the same time He filled the Lord's place. They found God in Him, as they had found God in the Lord; His presence made them God's very temples. The Name of Father, Son, and Holy Spirit, into which Christians were baptised, was found in actual experience to be one and the same Name. Thus it is out of the fulness of their own experience that the Apostles ever speak. Monotheists they remain without any qualification, but, as Dr. Wace has said: "It is their habitual and natural language to speak of the Lord Jesus Christ and of the Holy Spirit in the same terms and in the

---

* "The Church did not infer the divineness of the salvation from the divinity of the Saviour, as modern Christians often think that they must do: it inferred the divinity of the Saviour from the divineness of the salvation. Neither did it argue that God must be found in Jesus because He is there: it inferred that God is in Jesus because He is there so gloriously found. We prove the divinity of Christ: they beheld it. We have fallen back on intellectual methods: they built on spiritual experience."—W. N. Clarke, *The Christian Doctrine of God.*

same associations as those in which they speak of
God."* Throughout their writings the Lord is the
object of faith, and not merely the example of it;
and, if the same is not so obviously true of the Holy
Spirit, that is because His relation to ourselves as
the Inspirer of our faith and devotion makes it
less natural to think of Him as the object of our
faith also. Again and again the Apostles in their
writings pass from One Person to Another of the
Blessed Trinity in a way which shows that, while
on the one hand they distinguish Them, on the
other they adopt the same attitude towards all
Three. The well-known words, " The grace of the
Lord Jesus Christ, and the love of God, and the
communion of the Holy Ghost, be with you all,"
are simply the most familiar example of a fact plain
to every student of the New Testament. Everywhere we see plainly that it is facts upon which
they are resting, and not speculation. If St. John
makes a passing reference to the philosophic
doctrine of the Divine " Word," he derives nothing
from it; he employs it simply to express the
conclusion which the Lord's actual life and work
had forced upon him. Christians in later days
have often argued for the doctrine of the Trinity
upon philosophic grounds,† and there are minds to
which such arguments make a real appeal. But
such arguments are unknown to the writers of the

* Cf. Wace, *Christianity and Morality*, Series II., Lecture vii. The
writer of this paper is greatly indebted to that admirable book.

† The main philosophical argument arises from the difficulty of
conceiving of God as a " living God," if we deny the existence of real
distinctions in His interior life. Eternal love seems to require an eternal
object of love, eternal thought an eternal object of thought, and eternal
will an eternal product of that will. If in order to rid ourselves of this

New Testament; their reliance is upon facts—we might almost* say upon facts alone. It is just because God in His Son and in His Spirit has drawn so near to us that something of the mystery of His interior life has come within our view.

But then the Englishman will say, that it is not the language of the New Testament to which he takes exception, nor indeed to the ordinary devotional language which the Church employs in her hymns, her doxologies, and other such expressions of her mind. Such language, he fully recognises, is the natural language of religious experience— of the religious experience of the Apostles—and in measure, he hopes, of his own also. *Omnia exeunt in mysterium*, and it is foolish to quarrel with facts because we find a difficulty in fully accounting for them. His objection is that the Church seems to require him to go behind the facts, and to accept an elaborate theory as to the nature of God in order to account for them. He does not object to the doctrine of the Trinity as he finds it in the Athanasian Creed on the ground that it is a bad theory, but on the ground that it is an unnecessary one, and that no means exist for its verification. Now it is just at this point that the Englishman by no fault of his own misunderstands the Church's language. Individual teachers of the Church have propounded theories as to the interior life of God, but the Church does not ask our acceptance of

difficulty we regard the world as eternal, we make God dependent for the fullness of His life upon the world, and are thus involved in overwhelming difficulties of a different kind. Such arguments, however, appeal as little to the ordinary English mind as they would have appealed to the Hebrew.

* Almost, because the New Testament writers do also refer to the language of the Old Testament to support their faith—*e.g.* in Heb. i.

any one of them. The so-called doctrine of the
Trinity, as we find it most fully expressed in the
Athanasian Creed, is, like the so-called " laws "
of nature, not so much a theory to account for
the facts of experience, as a convenient summary
of the facts of experience themselves. The impression which the Athanasian Creed commonly
makes upon the mind is due, partly to the use of
words which sound like the language of an exact
science, and partly to the fact that the author, in
the careful balancing of his clauses, seems, like
the guide at the Hampton Court maze, to be sur-
veying from a loftier standpoint than our own the
territory of which he speaks, and to be directing
us moment by moment whether to turn to the
right hand or to the left. The history of Christian
doctrine, however, plainly shows that the impression
thus made upon us is an erroneous one. A short
explanation will make this clear. The Athanasian
Creed simply asserts the facts we have already
considered, while adding nothing to them.

Let us consider, firstly, the language employed.
To say that we worship One God as a Trinity, and
the Trinity as a Unity, is simply to assert the
revealed fact of the unity of Father, Son, and Holy
Spirit, without in any way attempting to explain
it. To say that we must not confound, or confuse,
the Persons simply means that, as the revealed
facts declare, we must not regard Father, Son, and
Holy Spirit as merely three different names for
one and the same God. The word " Person " is
a most unfortunate word, but it is difficult to suggest
any other to take its place which would not be
equally unfortunate. Human language fails us

when we try to describe the facts of our own nature ; it is worse than inadequate when we try to describe the facts of God's. The Church does not mean that Father, Son, and Holy Spirit are distinguished One from Another as human persons are distinguished ; the facts themselves forbid such a view. On the contrary, so perfect is their unity that, as St. Basil says : " If any one truly receive the Son, he will find that He brings with Him, on the one hand, the Father, on the other, the Holy Spirit. For neither can He be severed from the Father Who is ever of and in the Father : nor again disunited from His own Spirit Who operates all things by means of It." * The word " Person " has no definable meaning. There are three— what shall we say ? Perhaps, when we know as we are known, we may fill the blank. Meanwhile the word " Person " is like the x in algebra; it stands for what is to us unknown. † So it is also with the word " Substance." To say that we must not divide the substance means that the Divine attributes, as we know them, belong alike to Father, Son, and Holy Spirit, and this, as we have seen, is a fact of experience. But what the substance, or reality, of God, in all its greatness may be, the Church neither knows nor claims to know. So once more with the words " begotten " and " proceeding," which are used to describe the relation of the Son and of the Spirit

---

* Quoted by Bishop Forbes, *Explanation of the Nicene Creed*, p. 82.

† The Church does not even assert that Father, Son and Holy Spirit are to be distinguished in the same way, but only that they are to be distinguished. If, *e.g.*, any one wishes to maintain that the Holy Spirit's distinction from the Son is less marked in experience than the Son's distinction from the Father, it is quite open to him to do so.

M

respectively to the Father. The Church attaches
to these words no deep philosophical significance,
nor presumes to say in what precisely the meaning
of the one differs from the meaning of the other ;
she borrows them from the simple and popular
language of Scripture itself. To say that the Son
is " not made, nor created, but begotten " is but
to say that, though in His eternal being our Lord
is no part of the created universe, His relation to
the Father is one of Sonship and dependence. To
say that the Holy Ghost is " neither made, nor
created, nor begotten, but proceeding," is simply
to reproduce the Lord's language. It is to say
that He proceeds from God to us as from an ever-
living fountain, even as He takes us with Him back
to God.

" From the great deep to the great deep He goes."

In all this there is nothing technical, nothing
added to the revealed facts. The Christian Englishman believes every word of it. And if, to pass to
his second difficulty, the author of the Creed seems
unduly pontifical in his attitude towards us, we
should observe that his balanced clauses do not
claim any knowledge which the revealed facts
themselves do not yield. All that he really does
is to illustrate the formula, " Neither confounding
the Persons, nor dividing the Substance," by
applying it to the revealed attributes of God. If
he says of the Son and of the Spirit as of the Father
that Each is uncreated and incomprehensible and
eternal—incomprehensible here means not to be
contained in any portion of space—if again he
says that Each is Almighty and that Each is Lord,

that is merely to draw out for simple minds what is meant by saying that Each is God.

We may then boldly affirm that the Athanasian Creed itself is a monument of that respect for facts and dislike for abstract speculation which the Church shares with the Christian Englishman. We may add that the Church gives it to us just in order that, as the Englishman desires, we may have a religion of the heart, and not of the head. Is that mere paradox ? On the contrary, it is the simple truth. Had the Church wished us to have a religion of the head, she would never have insisted upon the doctrine of the Trinity, or given us the Athanasian Creed. The intellect finds the doctrine extremely difficult, and the intellect does not love what is difficult ; it desires something beneath it that it can grasp from top to bottom, not something far above it, which it can only dimly apprehend. There are those in our own day, as there were also in the early centuries, who are what we call intellectualists. Their powers of intellect are considerable, while their religious sense, their powers of contemplation and of worship, are little developed, and they prefer rather to exercise the powers which they have than to seek after those which they have not. What is their attitude towards this doctrine, and towards the Creed which especially enshrines it ? Mystery, which feeds the religious sense, is an offence to the intellect, and the intellectualist is always disposed to explain it away. Formerly he tended towards Unitarianism ; to-day he tends rather towards what the Athanasian Creed calls " confounding the Persons." He speaks of finding God in the

order and beauty of the world, in the life of Jesus
Christ, and in the heart of man, as if there were no
distinctions known to us within the life of God,
but only a Unity, which through different means
we dimly apprehend. That is, of course, to explain
the doctrine away, and those who do so naturally
show a strong dislike for the Athanasian Creed.
But the Church gives it to us not because of its
appeal to the mind, but because of the power of
the truth which it proclaims over the heart and the
life. To believe that "the Son is God" is to
believe that He Who lived our human life, and died
our human death, was God Himself come down
to us, God Himself entering into all our human
experience, to suffer with us and to suffer for us.
To believe that "the Holy Ghost is God" is to
believe that the Voice which speaks in our souls
to-day is no mere natural conscience of our own, but
God Himself dwelling in us, God Himself interesting
Himself in every one of us, God Himself striving
with all our wilfulness and sin, God Himself never
resting till all His high purpose for us is fulfilled.
There is no other belief, there never has been any
other belief, able to touch the heart like this. It
is God's love, God's sympathy, God's sacrifice of
Himself, that touch and that win us. If we do
not believe in the Divinity of the Son and of the
Holy Spirit, there is nothing left that will touch
us and win us in the same way. The Church does
not teach these doctrines simply because they are
useful ; she teaches them because the facts have
shown them to be true. But she insists upon
them as she does because they lead to a religion
of the heart and of the life, while their denial or

neglect leads to nothing of the kind. What says experience ? Shall we look at the Mission Field ? Roman Catholics are there; Anglicans and Russians are there; Presbyterians, Moravians, Wesleyans are there; believers in the Trinity of every country and of every class are there at work for God, living for Him, dying for Him. Where are those who reject or sit loose to the doctrine ? They are not very prominent in Christian evangelisation.

One point more, and that not as to the doctrine itself, but as to the Athanasian Creed. Has the Church any quarrel with the Englishman's conviction that it is what we are and do that matters ? Certainly not. The closing words of the Creed are most clear upon the point. But do not the miscalled " damnatory clauses " contradict them ? Let us see. If those clauses shock our conscience and our reason, it is because we misunderstand them. Let us observe that we are concerned with what the Creed means, and not with what it may have meant when it was written. It is given to us for our acceptance not by the Church of some other day, but by the Church of our own day, and its meaning is the meaning which the Church now gives to it. Did the so-called damnatory clauses ever mean that we should perish everlastingly as a punishment for refusing the teaching of the Church ? We do not know the author of the Creed, and still less do we know his exact meaning. But the Church of the West, in the fifth century and for long after, had mainly to deal with barbarians who had the minds of children, and she undoubtedly attached an importance to intellectual docility which does not normally belong to it. This question, however, is of no practical interest to-day. Whether or not this was once the Church's meaning, it is not her meaning now. Not only the English Church, but the Roman Church also, fully recognise that God does not hold us responsible for unbelief or misbelief which is not our own fault. What, then, is it that these clauses mean to-day ? They warn us, firstly, that we are all to some extent responsible for what we believe. Not only are we responsible for honest investigation, but in all belief worthy of the name the will has its part to play. Faith involves to some extent a leap in the dark, which on adequate grounds it is our duty to make. The clauses warn us, secondly, that what we are and do cannot be separated from our intellectual convictions ; belief arouses emotion and desire, and desire issues in action and in character. But there is more than this. Christian faith brings union with God through Christ, and with it the transformation both of action and of character. Let us approach the truth by an illustration. Suppose that a statesman is arguing for National Service in these days of crisis. He will tell us that without it we " cannot be saved," and that if Germany works her will with the British Empire, " without doubt it will perish ever-lastingly." Do we say that the statesman is intolerably harsh, and that he destroys the effect of the advice he gives by his deplorable damnatory clauses ? Do we suppose that he is maintaining the absurdity that the loss of our Empire will be a judgment upon us for the enormity of differing from him in opinion ? On the contrary, the loss, if it comes, will result from our policy of drift. There is one question, and only one. Is what he says true ? If it is not, he has no right to say it ; if it is, he has no right not to say it. The Church of God to-day speaks as he speaks, and means what he means. We perish everlastingly, if we perish, because of what we are and have done ; to reject the Creed only cuts us off from the remedy. What would we have the Church say ? The question whether we shall or shall not perish everlastingly is the question whether we have or have not eternal life. Eternal life is the gift of God. The Church knows no way to it, we ourselves know no way to it, except to receive it from Christ our Lord, nor of any way to receive it even from Him without faith in Him and self-surrender to His Holy Spirit, and such faith, such self-surrender, as are necessary can be given rightly only to our God. Perhaps we do not like this. But had we not better pay attention to the facts of our position ? Sin and eternal life are incompatible. How do we propose to get rid of our sin, and, having done so, lay hold of " the life which is life indeed " ? Can we do it without our Lord and His Spirit ? Can we do it without keeping our faith in Them " whole and undefiled " ? If we can, we need not trouble about the Athanasian Creed. On that happy morning when we wake to find sin dead within us by our own efforts, and eternal life attained, the Athanasian Creed will be dead also. Till then it lives—lives not to curse us, but to bless us, by pointing us to that living God, that holy, blessed, and glorious Trinity, Who alone can deal with our case.

But then we say : " Can we bear to believe

this? What of those who know not our Faith, or who, knowing it, honestly disbelieve it? Do we condemn them to eternal loss by accepting the Athanasian Creed?" No, we do not. Let us listen to our Lord's words. "If any man"— there is no exception—"willeth to do God's will, he shall know of the teaching whether it be of God, or whether I speak from Myself." If the Lord says, "Except ye believe that I am He, ye shall die in your sins," He says also that there is no one, in however black a darkness wandering, if only he wills in his inmost heart to do God's will, who will not ultimately attain to faith. Stern He might be to those who had seen and heard Him, God's perfect revelation, and yet refused to believe. He will not be equally stern to those who have heard only His servants to-day, with all our ignorance and misrepresentation of Him and of His Father. Though we ourselves fail, He has not necessarily failed. No man will ever perish by another's fault; no man will ever be lost whom God's love can save. Somehow—somewhere—some day—the Lord will seek out His own sheep, and " deliver them out of all places whither they have been scattered in the cloudy and dark day." Only—he who wills to do God's will must strive to know whether the message of the Church is true. St. John assures us that the witness which he bears is " the witness of God." "He that believeth not God hath made Him a liar; because he hath not believed in the witness that God hath borne concerning His Son." The evidence for the Christian faith was, St. John felt, so plainly God-given that no one could reject it without giving

God the lie. Can we will to do God's will if we do not examine it ? That is our challenge to England to-day. The doctrine of the Trinity is not a difficulty in the way of accepting the Christian faith and the Christian life. Rightly understood, it is an integral part of the one and the necessary foundation of the other.

XI

THE CHURCH

" The Holy Catholick Church:"

LOYALTY to the Church is essential **to** Christian living. Yet no notion is more deeply disliked. Often it is rejected in the name of a pure Christianity. The word "ecclesiastical" suggests repulsive conventionality. Similar taunts are now levelled at those who hold a high moral ideal. Therefore they disturb us less.

An Unmediated Religion—not Christianity

First comes the claim for an unmediated religion. The vital fact, it is said, is the experience of the mystic—"the flight of the alone to the alone." Church, priesthood, sacraments, are external. Those who regard them are formalists. They act as screens between the soul and God. The religion here suggested may be magnificent, but it is not Christian. We may grant that the soul has immediate communion with God. But this cannot

PREFATORY NOTE.—This paper is not a complete treatise on the Church. In regard to the illustrations used, they must not be taken as exact parallels. They serve only to make clearer certain parts of the argument. I have added a short list of books of moderate compass dealing with the subject.

J. N. F.

be identified with the historical Jesus of Nazareth —except through some kind of mediation. Even if we put aside all ecclesiastical institutions, we should need the New Testament. How else can we make any connexion between the light within and the Gospel of Jesus Christ ? The New Testament is itself a social product—the creature of the early Church.

But, further, if you carry your dislike of mediation to its conclusion, you can have no faith in Christ as Mediator. Those who object to the Church because it interferes with immediate communion are logically driven to repudiate the Saviour. Historically, that is what they do.

THE INVISIBLE CHURCH

Many do not go so far as this. The New Testament is too strong for them to reject all idea of Churchmanship. How can any one do this who reads the Acts or the Epistles ? The cynic may note a " deplorable drop " from the maxim " love your neighbour " to " love the brotherhood." Such a view is impossible to any one who pays regard to St. Paul's oft-repeated phrase about the Church as " the body of Christ," still more to the final pictures in the Apocalypse.

If the Church be " the fulness of Him that filleth all in all," we shall not get the full Christian character apart from it. So much is now recognised. Then these high terms about the Church are made ground to deny the claims of any Church we see. She is holy, " without spot or wrinkle," " the bride of Christ." Very good. The actual Church is full of corruption. Many of its members do not even try for the Christian ideal. These cannot be "the peculiar people, the royal nation, the holy priesthood." These high titles can attach only to the "saved." The Church we see is a caricature of the true Church. To that, and that alone, applies the language of the New Testament. That body is invisible. It is that society, "unknown and unknowable" to us, which is made up of the true children of God on their road to heaven. This doctrine of an invisible Church is not very popular now. It involves contradictions. Certain bonds, subtler than we know, do unite those striving for the same end in many different societies. But we cannot fairly speak of a social life of this kind. No corporate body can act as such, if it be entirely unrecognisable. It is better to discard the term "Church" than to employ it in this way.

THE CHURCH AND THE KINGDOM

The argument for the visible Church was condensed in "*Ecce Homo*"—in the words : "Did Christ die for a metaphor ? " In other words, Was all the preaching of the Kingdom meaningless ? If our Lord had a message only for individuals, and no will to gather them into a flock, why did He talk about the Kingdom and pray that they might be one ? True, He used the term "Church" very little. Yet His claim to be Messiah involved it. The Messiah is the long-expected Redeemer of the Hebrew people. The Church is the Jewish Kingdom consummated. We are the "Israel of God." Disraeli used to call the Christian Church the one effective Jewish institution. Our Lord in founding the Apostolic college, the assembly in the upper room, the Pentecostal outpouring and its results, the whole life of early Christians pictured in the New Testament, show us a visible society with developing institutions. They do not show us isolated individuals, converted, and then making a union of convenience.

LOVE AND SOCIAL UNITY

The teaching of Jesus Christ involves this inevitably. Love is a social grace. If God be Love, and if human nature be formed to respond to Him, you cannot have pure individualism. Love is the secret of all reality. Our nature cannot fulfil itself in isolation. We can realise ourselves only by going out of ourselves. Personality implies society. This is shown by the way in which, nowadays, the most extreme opponents of Christ deny that Love is the law either for God or man.

THE CHURCH AND HUMAN SOCIETY

The Church is supernatural in origin and aim. It is not unnatural. This truth of human nature governs all right thinking about politics. Each man has his own individuality; but fellowship is the law of his being. The isolated man is inconceivable. He would not be human; he would have no "language but a cry." This is not a discovery of Christianity. Long before, it was said that man is a political animal—*i.e.* social life is of the essence of his being. At no moment is he alone. His birth ushers him into a society.

He could not be reared without it. Even the exaggerated individualism of the day before yesterday was possible only by the force of a highly elaborate social system. Long since individualism has vanished from politics. No one now thinks of the State as a contractual union between self-subsistent individuals, with no end but immediate utility. It is known as a common life, in which all share, moulding it, and being moulded by it. That is why loyalty is due to it—and sacrifice. Herein lies the difference between a true and a false notion of the Church. Does a man first become a Christian, and afterwards pick out for his convenience a society which suits him, and leave it when it does not ? Or is he a Christian because he is a baptised member of that society which began in the upper room ? We cannot read the New Testament and hold any other view than the latter—at least of the past. It is now admitted by those who do not hold it. To make their attack plausible they seek to discredit the New Testament.

When we speak of Christianity we are speaking of a definite historical phenomenon. To adopt Christianity does not mean merely to accept certain ideals. It means to join the Church. The Church to us is the central fact in the spiritual experience of the race. To be a member of it is to live in touch with all its members, dead and living. The Church includes both. In the terms of art, she is militant here on earth, but in union with that larger part which is triumphant " beyond our bourne of time and space." How far the term " Christian " may be fitting to denote a certain

individual attitude irrespective of any society we
need not inquire. That is not what it does mean.
To be a Christian is to be a member of the Church,
just as to be an Englishman is to be a subject of
King George.

THE INCARNATION AND THE CHURCH

All this is congruous with the Incarnation.
Objections to the Church and the sacraments
lead logically to a denial of that truth. The
Incarnation tells us that we have not to worship
God in abstraction. He entered into human life,
submitting to its limitations. The Church is the
continued expression of that life. She is called
the body of Christ, " the fulness of Him that filleth
all in all." It is the fulfilling, the development of
the life of Jesus under earthly conditions. So well
known are these words that we take them for
granted. Westcott defines the body " as the
expression of the life in terms of the environment."
The Church is that society which is the means of
the active and continued work of Jesus Christ
in this world—*i.e.* JESUS CHRIST IS THE
MEANING OF THE CHURCH.

THE CHURCH HOLY

That is why we call it Holy. Many people
cavil at this. How can the Church as we see it be
called Holy ? This feeling, as we saw, was partly
the ground for the theory of an Invisible Church.
The Church, it was agreed, is described as Holy in
the New Testament. This is not true of many
individuals in it. It seemed, then, better to use

the term "Church" for something other than the actual concrete body. This is an error due to misconception of the nature of corporate life. Holiness is the end of the Church. In so far as she fulfils her object she is Holy. That is what she is always tending to be—even in times of corruption. Evidence of this is to be found in the revivals of the Church. These are more wonderful than her conquests. The greatest miracle in social history is the recuperative power of the Church. Strong convictions may readily win territory in a rush. Proof of life is given in the power to hold it against counter-attacks and to recover lost ground.

The Holiness of the Church is not the perfection of all its members, but the moulding force of the supernatural life of the Spirit in the whole society. This life is communicated in the sacraments.

Another evidence of this Holiness is the nature of some recent attacks. Formerly men assailed the Church for hypocrisy. They said that she was not living up to her ideals. This is true. So long as men are sinful, there will be a gap between what we are and what we want to be. The gap will be greatest where the ideal is highest. Now the boot is on the other leg. Men attack the Church on account of her ideal, not on account of its failure. Once we were wrong because we were not altogether successful, now we are wrong in so far as we are. Holiness, as defined by Christians— chastity, humility, self-denial, the "fruits of the Spirit" in St. Paul's phrase, are the target of scorn. The ideal is said to be decadent and unmanly. This attack could have no meaning were there not a sense in which the Church is rightly called " Holy."

THE CHURCH ONE

So it is with Christ's Church. The Church is One. How can that be true ? We see her " by schisms rent asunder." Between English, Roman, and Russian Christians is there any unity save that of the Invisible Church ? On consideration we can see such unity, though imperfect. The structure is the same and the fundamental bonds. The Creed, the Sacraments, an ordained ministry under Episcopal government are common. Bodies who hold to these things tend to have certain qualities not found elsewhere. There is a freemasonry between people of a similar education independent of their actual school or college. Moreover, little as we may see it, we present a certain common front to the adversary. Attacks upon the Creed, upon the supernatural, upon the external forms, upon an Episcopally ordained ministry touch us all. Through these attacks more perfect union may come. The enemy will press us together— just as the Germans have consolidated the British Empire. Schism, we must bear in mind, is a rent inside the Church. A child is baptised a member of Christ, not of any particular Church. Once more, constitutional unity does not now exist. It is far more feasible among those who have the same constitutional structure. Its chief obstacle is that structural addition, the autocratic Papacy, which depresses the episcopal order in a large part of the Church.

N

The Church Catholic

Somewhat similar is the problem aroused by the word "catholic." That means universal. Clearly the Church does not include the whole world. Many have not heard of it. Many who know its claims reject them. Again, it is said that if we want to make the Church universal, we ought to do away with all dogmatic tests. Many men have the religious spirit who could not say the Creeds. Some of them do not believe in God. Why do we exclude such men—devoted, thoughtful, high-minded ? The answer is twofold. (1) If the Catholic Church is to exist at all it must have some meaning. To state that meaning is to lay down a Creed. So long as men are free they will not all accept it. Except by persecution, or a unanimity which we cannot foresee in a sinful world, the Church cannot embrace every one. There is nothing about which men are unanimous. Even if the Church meant no more than the religion of humanity, that could not make it universal. The ideal of humanity is passionately rejected by some. (2) Secondly, what is proposed is a new test, the test of temperament. It is true that the religious temperament is independent of dogma. That temperament is far from being universal. If the Catholic Church be taken to be the society of all persons of religious feeling, whatever they think, it would still remain a partial, exclusive body. The most arbitrary and aristocratic of all societies is a religious body with no bond but temperamental sympathy.

The Church is Catholic because she appeals to

(*a*) all men, (*b*) the whole of man. No limits of race, or sex, or age, or colour, or status affect membership. " There is neither Jew nor Greek, male nor female, barbarian, Scythian, bond nor free ; but Christ is all and in all." The Church meets the universal need for redemption to eternal life. The fact that some do not realise their need does not hinder the universality of her appeal. Also, she is Catholic because she appeals to the whole of man—body, soul and spirit. No instinct, no emotion, no faculty is left out—where it does not involve sin. Every part of human life in society it consecrates. It does not appeal to the inward only, but also to the outward. The Incarnation and the Sacraments are the charter of her liberties, and save her from the false spirituality which seeks God merely in abstraction. She has a place for politics, for law, for commerce, for industry, for the athlete and the labourer, the lover and the child, no less than for the thinker, the poet, the preacher or the monk.

The Church the Home of Sinners

Only as we bear this in mind can we get a right orientation. Nowadays people think of the Church as a club of religious people, the society of the respectable. Worse still, many Churchpeople think this of themselves. It is the polar opposite of the truth. The Church is Catholic because she is the home of sinners. Her claim is that none is so low but the blood of Christ can redeem him ; none so high but he needs God's forgiving love. Good Churchmen, in their smugness, get most harm from the error of the Church " select," the company of the " moral gentlemen." Many also are kept outside because they do not feel good enough. We need the Church, just as we need the body and blood of our Lord, not because we are good, but because we are not. We must get back to the idea that the Church is, above all things, a body of penitents. The Roman Church, with all its faults, has never lost this. Nor does she make the mistake of expecting from all the same level of devotion. Puritanism is by its very idea the root of the opposing error. Even now this dominates English religion, and that among many who scorn the Puritan virtues. Many a so-called " Catholic " congregation hugs itself in this delusion.

Baptism

That is why the mark of membership is, above all, an outward rite. The Church as a definite, visible body must have some recognisable mode of entry. A sense of goodness, of being saved, could not give such a mark. It would throw us back on individual feeling. Even a collective judgment about conversion would be dangerous—alike to those whom it kept in and to those whom it kept out. The mode of entry instituted by our Lord has never been changed—*Holy Baptism*. Hostility is still aroused at the assertion that this outward ordinance can make any one a " member of Christ." It is said to be unspiritual, mechanical. This objection is due, firstly, to that false spiritualism which banishes God from the world. Logically it leads to denial of the Incarnation. A second cause is the lack of understanding of Christianity as life in a society.

SOCIAL INITIATION

Baptismal Regeneration is mere matter of fact. No one who joins any society is precisely the same person as he was before. What the Church teaches is this : (1) A change has been effected in the newly baptized ; (2) that change means the life of the Holy Ghost within him. If the Church be the sphere of the operation of the Holy Ghost no less can be true. Whatever be the vital principle of the Christian society, it is now within him. Consider what happens when any one is initiated into any society, a school or college, a club, regiment, trade union, Freemasons' lodge. He is changed. The life of the society begins to permeate him. He begins to have new interests, new thoughts, new hopes, new enmities, new capacities. In proportion to the greatness of the society and its more or less all-embracing character this new life tends to make him a new person. A new boy at a public school, a freshman at college, changes vastly in a week. At first he is far from being a typical product of the society. The shaping process must be gone through. At the end some imbibe more, some less, of its spirit. Yet all are changed by it—even those who protest against it. Yet from the first he feels that it belongs to him. The portraits of dead worthies inspire him. Its triumphs are his glory. Its little troubles make his gloom. An instance to-day would be a new subaltern in the Black Watch. He is proud with a new pride—sometimes a little ludicrous to his friends. He is more than he was; no longer a mere individual, but breathing " the power of an endless life."

For a Christian this change is wrought by Holy Baptism. *Christ is the meaning of the Church.* In being united to it, its spirit enters into him. He cannot help this. The Church is the society of the redeemed. The newly baptized is living in a new world. He is a new creature, the scion of a new race. What he will make of this life is doubtful. So it is doubtful what he will make of his life as a member of his own family or an Englishman. But he is not the same as he was before. To deny the grace of Baptism is to assert that he is the same. This is contrary to common sense. This error comes of looking at grace as a quantity, a substance. Grace means God acting upon the soul. The grace of Baptism is the communicating of the new life of this great society, which is the terrestrial expression of Jesus Christ. That is why we pray that the Holy Ghost may sanctify this water to the mystical washing away of sin—*i.e.* to remove the child from the natural sphere into the supernatural and to make him a " member of Christ, the child of God, and an inheritor of the Kingdom of Heaven." Baptism gives him letters of naturalisation in the " city which hath foundations." He is justified— *i.e.* God sees him not as he is, but as he shall be— just as a mother thinks of her son not as the schoolboy he was, but as the scholar he will be. His is now a part " of the inheritance of the saints." In every case the gift of life is there. In those in whom it is stifled the supernatural life makes return easier.

THE REAL PRESENCE

This life so begun must be nourished. The sacramental principle is involved first in the Incarnation, then in the Church as a society functioning here but with all its meaning beyond. It is focussed in the Sacraments. The sacramental use of objects is common in human affairs. It is the principle of badges, colours, uniforms, money, flags, ensigns of royalty—*i.e.* we give to things a meaning and a value far different from their material purpose. They are something different— the royal standard is not what an untaught savage would think it, a pretty piece of silk with various colours in an odd pattern. The policeman's hand uplifted in the street is a symbol of the power of the British Empire and the course of all British history. These things must be borne in mind when we come to discuss the Eucharist. Scorn is heaped upon those who maintain the real presence of our Lord in the Sacrament of the altar. We cannot here do more than say a word or two, avoiding technical phrases. What we ask of any believer in the Incarnation and the Church is this : Can we deem the elements of bread and wine consecrated to the gift of Life to be unchanged by that ? A thing is what it means. Are the consecrated elements no more than common bread and wine after they have been set apart by the public prayers of the Church speaking through its ordained minister and in unison with our Lord's words on the eve of the Passion ? Some do think that there is no differ- ence. This comes of lack of appreciation of social institutions, and of a hard-and-fast way of regarding the outward world. These errors will grow less as men understand a little better the implications of corporate life and the infinite changefulness of material things. It is not the Real Presence but the denial of it that is due to an extravagantly mechanical notion of the world. Let us take an illustration. A piece of paper with " Pay So-and-so five pounds " written on it is worth nothing. Add to it the signature of a man with credit at his bank, and it becomes something different—money. How ? Only by virtue of complex social arrangements. He must have credit. The bank must be solvent. Even when you have the notes you cannot turn them into gold unless the Bank of England is solvent. That depends on the credit of the country. Gold itself is made legal tender by an Act of Parliament. Its purchasing power varies— *e.g.* it is less now by a good deal than it was before the war. The real value of that piece of paper depends, then, on an intricate combination of social facts. But given all these things, the signature turns a piece of paper into money.* Similar is the change effected at consecration. Behind it lies : (1) The history of the Church ; (2) the original institution by its Founder ; (3) the competence of the priest.

THE CHRISTIAN MINISTRY

That brings us to the problem of the ministry. Clearly this cannot be discussed at length. This much may be said. Only a low view of grace and of the Eucharist can be satisfied with vague notions

* For the correctness of treating cheques as money, see Sidgwick's " Principles of Political Economy."

about the ministry. If Christianity be a special kind of social life, the Church must have some official representation. Then the moment you have officials you have the danger of officialism. Clericalism may be the enemy. That is no reason for discarding a clergy.

THE CHURCH APOSTOLIC

The Church is Apostolic, as well as Catholic. What claims our loyalty is the society that has developed in unbroken continuity since the Apostles. Apart from individual inspiration we have no means whereby we may be assured of the genuineness of grace. God came to us in Jesus of Nazareth. He comes to us in His Church through a ministry that has come down from Him and is no mere creature of our will. Orders in the Church can be discerned very early. They have gone on ever since. For fifteen centuries this position was not seriously questioned. That ought to be enough for us. All the baptized belong to the Catholic Church. We have no call to condemn other bodies of Christians. But we need not hesitate about our own loyalty to the developed order of the Christian community. If the Church be the central fact in the spiritual experience of the race, the great witness to the unity of history, we shall do well to pause before we throw away any element of its age-long inheritance. Even where this is needful, it is not done without loss. That prophecy should arise independently, and sometimes in rebuke of the official element is what we should expect. The unworthiness of officials does not invalidate their public acts in the Church any more than it does in the State. Those who speak as though it did have not thought out the meaning of the public corporate character of Church life. A priest does not mean a specially good man, but a man set apart for public functions in the Church. What may be the relation of the Catholic Church to those bodies of baptized Christians who repudiate her immemorial system we cannot discuss. Charity must never fail. We may treat them as unauthorised guilds, since they are certainly Christian and equally certainly organic bodies. Charity may at times approve dispensation from some disciplinary rule. *Yet this can only be if the need of rules be recognised.* Claims are sometimes made that the Church, being the symbol of Love, ought to do without rules. All conditions of membership —theological, institutional and moral—are treated as hampering to the free spirit of love. If the Church is a society this claim cannot be allowed. Legalism is an evil no less than it was when our Lord fought it among the Jews. The evils of legalism do not do away with the need of law. Law of some sort there must be. General rules guiding the members of the Christian society and establishing its official acts are inherent in the nature of corporate religion. Law, however, is a rough formula. We must beware of a narrowly juristic conception of the Christian life. If so, all moral effort is satisfied with a minimum. We must beware no less of any notions of supreme legislative power in the Church of such a kind as practically to do away with the Kingship of Christ. But that the Church could remain a Church and yet be without authority over its individual members is contrary to the nature of things.

"I believe in the Holy Church" implies this. Or, to end as we began, "Loyalty to the Church is essential to Christian living." This is scouted because it means a recognition of authority. "I believe" implies trust. We cannot explain away this phrase as meaning no more than I believe in the existence of the Church.

CHURCH AUTHORITY

Church authority is a hard saying now. But it is the more needful. To the modern mind authority in any form is repugnant. A new platform for education is now vaunted, which is to remove all restraints from children, and never to teach the growing boy a lesson he does not like. So in regard to the Church. Not that there is a lack of religious feeling. On the contrary, it is rampant. "God is furiously in the fashion," said a Parisian dame. Religion, however, men take on this condition. It is to be what they like—Catholic, Evangelical, or Liberal. Outside the Church it clothes in a thousand many-coloured robes of fantasy the aspiring dreamers of high things. It is sincere but subjective and capricious. All this is contrary to Christianity. The very name Christ signifies authority from above. Lord has come to mean no more than a title. Men can speak of Jesus as Lord and mean nothing by it. But Lord means Master. The problem of authority in religion does not arise, as some do vainly talk, through the pretensions of aspiring prelates. It begins the

moment you call yourself a disciple of Christ.
You are not loyal to a leader if you follow him only
where you see that he is right. Loyalty means
that you follow him where you do not see, on
account of your belief in his insight. So it is in
regard to the Church. Belief in her authority
comes from your idea of human nature. If man
be only a rational individual, and social bonds
matters of convenience, then it is vain to talk of
authority. At most, authority would be only that
of the mathematical expert. His guidance all
can accept because we know that it is subject to
mechanical tests. Logical method works like
machinery. Given the premises, results are
certain.

HUMAN NATURE AND AUTHORITY

If, however, man be more than this; if his
being be compact of love and will no less than
intelligence; and if (as Christianity and true
politics alike teach) fellowship be of the essence of
personality, then there is real place for authority.
The spiritual experience of the race is concentrated
in the judgments of the Church. No one is wise to
neglect that. Yet here once more a caution is
needed. The temper of the exponent of authority
is not what is often supposed. A believer in
authority does not mean a man who wants to bully
other people, any more than a believer in freedom
means a man who wants to do what he likes. The
test of faith in liberty is willingness to allow it to
others. The test of faith in authority is submission to it ourselves. Here again we must
distinguish. The believer in Church authority is

no slave. He has not given his mind to some one else to do what he likes with. What happens is this. One of the most important factors in his judgment is the collective voice. On any topic on which the Church has a mind, he knows that it is less probable that that mind is in error than that he is so himself. Such a reminder is more needed by clever men than by stupid. Authority is not designed to oppress the everyday Christian. Rather it is a bulwark to protect him against the attacks of clever but onesided speculation. This is all that is done by a document so apparently elaborate as the Athanasian Creed. It guards the main truth, the supernatural revelation in Jesus Christ, against theories which if logically developed would destroy that truth. Also it asserts that the intellect of man belongs to his whole personality, and needs redemption no less than do other parts of his being.

AUTHORITY NOT ABSOLUTE

Deference to authority has regard to (*a*) past experience ; (*b*) the collective voice. A man should differ from it, where he must, only with the greatest reluctance. Yet authority is not absolute. In the last resort the Church must not override the individual conscience. Cases there are like that of Athanasius, when the individual by his courage to stand alone has saved the Church. Authority gives a very strong presumption. But she is not infallible. Nor can any authority, even that of God, be purely external. It must speak through the reason and conscience of the individual or it is not intelligible.

The Church Indefectible

If we have faith in Christ, we do indeed believe that the Church will be so far guided by the Holy Ghost that she will never deny the purpose of her being. This is in technical phrase to say that she is *indefectible*. That does not assert that her pronouncements are beyond criticism. It is almost universally admitted that the decisions of councils rest for their ultimate support on the general acceptance of the Church.

Authority must not Generate mere Conservatism

One more caution is needed. Regard for authority does not mean mere conservatism. Experience is always fresh. History does not repeat itself. No new problems are identical with old ones. Just now men scorn tradition. The world is new, they say. New methods, new ideas are wanted. " Whatever is is wrong." Let us make the world afresh. Ah! you cannot do that. No man and no people can cut the painter which ties the ship of human life to its past. No age is entirely new. Indeed, if each age had really to start afresh we should always be in the primeval state—whatever that was. We should each of us have to evolve the rudiments of a language. Therefore we must regard the past, but we must not be ever slaves to it. Least of all must the Church be ruled by the "dead hand." "The problem is how to make ourselves the heirs of history without becoming its slaves." The Church of God is the great adventure. We cannot confine that to the age of the martyrs, or even to the romance of St. Francis. " Now is the day of salvation." Antiquarian sentiment has its place in religious no less than in national life. But that place is a lowly one.

Faith in the Church means faith in the Holy Ghost present. Opportunities greater than any in the past are now ours. The scene in front of us has more of wonder than all the beauties we have passed. But to reach it we need courage and a calm mind. The heroic temper will conquer as it always does. It has been the ill-fate of the Church of England that it has appealed too little to the sense of sacrifice, which is bound up strangely with the sense of newness. Let us look back, but only in order the better to leap forward.

O GOD of unchangeable power and eternal light, look favourably on Thy Church, that wonderful and sacred mystery ; and by the tranquil operation of Thy perpetual providence carry out the work of man's salvation ; and let the whole world feel and see that things which were cast down are being raised up, that those which had grown old are being made new, and that all things are returning to perfection through Him from Whom they took their origin, even through our Lord Jesus Christ.

SOME BOOKS OF REFERENCE

The Holy Catholic Church. H. B. Swete.
Christ and the Church. A. W. Robinson.
The Kingdom of Christ. F. D. Maurice.

Symbolism.   J. A. Möhler.
Have You understood Christianity?   W. J. Carey.
What is Catholicity?   T. A. Lacey.
The Marks of the Church.   Darwell Stone.
The Fellowship of the Mystery.   J. N. Figgis.
God's City.   H. S. Holland.
Creed and Character (Lectures III.–IX.).   H. S. Holland.

The Bibliography at the end of this volume should also be consulted.

XII

THE COMMUNION OF SAINTS

" The Communion of Saints."

BELIEF in the Communion of Saints may be
regarded as a corollary of belief in the Holy
Catholic Church. So soon, indeed, as it is
realised that the Church Universal, the brotherhood of the people of God, is not exhausted by
that minor outpost of the celestial army which
at any given moment in history is " militant here
in earth," but includes also those who have passed
into the unseen world and of whom we rightly speak
as " the majority," the idea of the Communion of
Saints becomes virtually identical with that of the
Church on its more mystical side. It is disputed,
indeed, among the learned as to whether the Latin
phrase *communio sanctorum*, as originally used,
meant properly " fellowship of consecrated people "
or " joint participation in holy things." Either
translation would fit the Latin : but these are the
very pedantries of scholarship. The value of the
clause as it stands in the Creed to-day is determined not by any nice arguings about its origin,
but by its effective function in the living experience
of the Christian Church. To believe in the
Communion of Saints is to live as one who is
conscious always of " a cloud of witnesses," the

O

" general assembly and church of the firstborn who are enrolled in heaven," and of our living unity with all those, of whatever age or country, who are citizens in that " heavenly Jerusalem " which is "the city of the living God "—the God Who, as our Lord Himself has taught us, " is not the God of the dead but of the living : for all live unto Him."

> " One family we dwell in Him,
> One Church above, beneath ;
> Though now divided by the stream—
> The narrow stream—of Death."

The author of the Epistle to the Hebrews speaks in one passage of " the spirits of just men made perfect " : in another he declares, with reference to the saints and heroes of old time, that their perfection cannot be realised apart from the perfection of those still upon the earth. " These all, having had witness borne to them through their faith, received not the promise, God having planned beforehand some better thing, which has to do with us, that apart from us they should not be made perfect."

There is truth in both points of view. We believe, indeed, that " the souls of the faithful, after they are delivered from the burden of the flesh, are in joy and felicity," that they are " with Christ, which is far better," that their life is one of growth towards perfection, and that in a relative sense the " spirits of just men " may be said to be already perfected. On the other hand, it follows, necessarily from the essentially social character of the Christian salvation and the unity of the Church that the bliss of any must be incomplete apart from the bliss of all. The Divine Kingdom is not yet realised in its fullness. "We see not yet all things subjected to Him." Christ Himself has not yet entered upon the complete fullness of His victory ; and what is true of Christ must be true also of those "many brethren " who are to be sharers of His throne.

There is a further point. Honesty compels the recognition that the majority even of those who in a real sense may be said to have departed this life in the faith and fear of Christ were yet at the time of their departure far indeed from the completeness of spiritual maturity and moral perfection which must belong to the "pure in heart " who are to enjoy that immediate vision of God which we call "Heaven." It fell recently to the lot of the writer to speak words of Christian consolation to a young soldier whose mother had died some years previously and who had just lost his father. His reply was : "Yes, sir : I know it's right, what you say : and I *know* my mother's gone to a good place. *I'm not so sure about my father.*" It is an obvious defect in the Burial Service of the Church of England that it appears *primâ facie* to suggest the immediate "joy and felicity " of *all* the faithful departed without discrimination. The tendency is carried still further in the sentimentalism of popular hymns. It may well be that death, as it is the supreme event, is also the most educative experience in a man's life : that those who have passed over into the unseen world have entered upon some new and overwhelming experience and revelation of God's love, which enables them to make more rapid advance in the life of the spirit and to grow towards perfection more speedily than was altogether possible on earth. We do not know. But it is in any case unreasonable to assume, with popular Protestantism, that the faithful departed are instantaneously made perfect, by a kind of arbitrary miracle, at the moment of death, and are forthwith to be regarded as being " in Heaven." There must surely be an Intermediate State, a " Purgatory."

Yet not a Purgatory in the debased mediæval sense which is popularly suggested by the term. I mean by Purgatory simply a condition of being purified from imperfection and from sinfulness : a state of continuous growth in the direction of holiness and of the love of God. In so far as the soul, in its growth towards God, comes to appreciate more truly both the love of God, and also the despite done to the Divine Love by its own past sins and failures to respond to Love's appeal, there must surely be involved in its purification an ever-deepening repentance for the past, an element of sorrow and of pain : yet inasmuch as there is also an ever-deepening knowledge of God as He truly is, an increase in understanding both of the beauty of holiness and of the splendour of Love Triumphant, the deepest element in the life of souls in " Purgatory " must assuredly be not pain or sorrow but rather an increasing happiness and joy—joy in God, and in the goodness and love and beauty of God—a sharing, indeed, in God's very life, of which " Heaven " itself is but the ideal consummation in a Church completed and redeemed. It was a true intuition which led St. Catherine of Genoa, in her treatise upon Purgatory, the teaching of which inspiredNewman in his poem, "The Dream of Gerontius," to lay emphasis upon *love* and not wrath as the unvarying determinant of the Divine attitude towards sinners. The soul, released from the trammels of its earthly body, " flies " (in the words of Newman's poem) " to the dear feet of Emmanuel," and forthwith becomes conscious, in overwhelming power, at once of the Redeemer's amazing love, and of its own inability to stand before the " keen sanctity " of His gaze. It is this, and this alone, which constitutes the element of pain in the purgatorial discipline which the repentant soul both claims and welcomes and rejoices to endure. It is well that we are to-day recovering within the Church of England some realisation of the spiritual truth and reality under-lying a conception of this kind. It is commonly recognised now that the reaction against mediæval doctrines of Purgatory which was characteristic of the reforming movement of the sixteenth century went too far : nor is the recognition confined to the representatives of any particular " school of thought." " Broad Churchmen " and " Evan-gelicals " of the younger type are increasingly at one with " Anglo-Catholics " and " High Church-men " in their perception of the need for a develop-ment of doctrine along these lines.

The crude division of all souls at death into the immediately " saved " and the immediately " lost " is in truth satisfactory neither to the Christian mind nor to the Christian heart. It is altogether too mechanical a conception to accord with the facts of life : it is too arbitrary a solution to be worthy of the character of God as Christ reveals Him. A great step forward is made when it is realised that in respect of all these matters we are

in a region of spiritual realities of which we can
have no exact knowledge. The literal truth of
what lies beyond the grave is hidden from us.
We know that all souls are in the hand of God.
We know that man has within him immortal
longings which can never find abiding satisfaction
in the life of earth. The resurrection of Jesus
Christ from the dead has assured us of the life of
the world to come. For the rest we are in the region
of allegory and symbol; and it is important not
to confuse symbols with the things symbolised.
We are constrained to operate with the conceptions
of "heaven" and "purgatory" and "hell";
but we know that "heaven" is not a place, but the
ideal consummation of eternal life in God, only to
be realised in its fullness in a fellowship of "many
brethren": that "purgatory" is but a name for
progress towards the heavenly state: that "hell"
is simply a pictorial symbol of the condition of a
soul so wholly self-identified with evil as to have
become finally incapable of life in God.

What, then, in the light of these ideas, are
we to think with regard to the present life and
condition in the unseen world of those whom in
this life we have loved and lost? We know that
"the souls of the righteous are in the hand of God."
We think of them as being increasingly *nearer* to
God: as being "with Christ, which is far better."
But what of their present relation to ourselves?
Is any effectual fellowship still possible between
the living and the "dead"? We profess indeed
in terms our faith in the communion of saints: but
it is to be feared that, wherever the influences of
Protestantism of the more rigorous type have

penetrated, belief in the communion of saints has largely failed to find any effectual means of expression in religious life and practice. It has remained, as a clause in the Creed, largely inoperative : it has not stood for any definite or concrete realisation of living fellowship between quick and dead.

The human heart craves for such a fellowship ; and the starvation of a legitimate spiritual craving, here as always, brings its inevitable nemesis. It cannot, surely, be unreal to trace a connexion between the absence from popular religion of any effectual realisation of the communion of saints, and the enormous vogue of spiritualism in modern times. Christianity, of course, has no interest in opposing itself to investigations undertaken in a genuinely scientific spirit and temper in *any* region of research, neither is it concerned to deny the inherent possibility of direct communications between the departed and the living. There are good Christians at the present time who are convinced that strange messages from the unseen world are occasionally vouchsafed—especially, perhaps, in periods of stress and crisis—for the comfort of those on the earth, and that the spirits of those who have passed from the scenes of this present strife have been known to manifest themselves unsought, and by mysterious intimations to reveal their presence to the living. So also there are many excellent Christians who are disposed to take seriously the proceedings of the Society for Psychical Research, and to look for further light, as the result of them, upon the problems of life and death. The present writer is unable to share their attitude; and, since it is not possible here to enter into an elaborate argument upon the subject, he must be allowed, without condemning others, to express his personal conviction that it is not given to man to penetrate, by methods of research analogous to those which govern the processes of physical science, into the mysteries which lie beyond death, and that it is to the spiritual intuitions of religious faith, rather than to any process of direct experiment, that we are to look for light upon these problems. Regarded from this point of view, the elaborate and inconclusive researches even of the most scientific investigators appear at best pathetically futile; while the proceedings of the baser spiritualism are in essence nothing more nor less than a revival, under modern conditions, of that illicit and demoralising necromancy which the Catholic Church of history has consistently, and in the writer's judgment rightly, condemned.

There is no adequate safeguard against error except truth. It is useless to attempt to combat the substitution of spiritualism for Christianity, or the proposal to combine the two, merely by negative cautions and vague warnings against superstition. The Church in these islands needs to recover the inheritance which is rightfully hers in the doctrine of the communion of saints, and to give practical expression, in her corporate religious life and teaching, to the corollaries of that doctrine. The matter is especially urgent at the present time, when by reason of the war half England is in mourning, when there is scarcely a household which has not lost son or brother or intimate friend. At no period in the nation's history has there been a more widespread yearning for some concrete realisation of our abiding unity in Christ with those who have been taken away from the scenes and relationships of this earthly life. The communion of saints, interpreted as a purely theoretical dogma, fails altogether to satisfy the hunger of men's hearts : it needs to be made vivid and actual as a living fellowship of quick and dead.

If we ask what form such a fellowship is to take, the answer must be that it can only take the form of a fellowship of mutual prayer. It is surely an inevitable corollary of the doctrine of the Church that her members pray for one another : nor is there any bond between human souls comparable to the knowledge that each remembers other in intercession before the throne of God. The activity of those whose life is hid with Christ in God is an activity directed consciously towards God on behalf of others in union with the prayer of Christ.*
Self-dedication towards God on behalf of others is both the inner meaning of intercessory prayer and also the essence of the Christian spirit : it is for this reason that Christ Himself is regarded in the New Testament as the supreme Intercessor on behalf of man. In proportion as those whom we have loved and lost are truly sharers in the unseen world in the life and the activity of Christ, we may be confident that their life is in its essence one of prayer on behalf of us their brethren who are " militant here on earth." Nor is it altogether

---

* Compare the saying, " I shall spend my heaven in doing good on the earth," attributed to the French Carmelite, Sister Teresa of the Child Jesus.

reasonable to suppose that they are denied the knowledge which is requisite to make their prayers intelligent. True it is that we are in large measure ignorant of the present conditions of their life. Such ignorance should at least have the effect of making us chary of dogmatising with regard to it in a negative sense. It has been supposed that God through the Spirit makes known to them the present circumstances and needs of those whom they love on earth. More recently it has been suggested that since Christ has not ceased to be incarnate, and since the Church has ever maintained the legitimacy of prayer addressed directly to the still human Christ, exalted in majesty at God's "right hand," Christianity must presuppose in the case of our Lord what can best be described as an extension of His human consciousness, whereby it is enabled to become universal in its scope and range. To hold that this is to be explained as due to a kind of merging of Christ's manhood in His deity is to capitulate in the end to the heresy technically called Eutychian; and by analogy it has been argued that in the case of the departed also, who are now sharers in the life of Christ, there may be in some measure a like extension of consciousness, whereby they are enabled to be aware of the things of earth with an immediacy of apprehension impossible to those who are still trammelled by the limitations of the flesh.

To some, doubtless, the speculation will appear unduly bold. They will prefer to take refuge in a present agnosticism, " until the day break and the shadows flee away." But there are others who will desire to go farther : they will desiderate some consideration of the practice known as the *invocation* of the saints, a practice which—at least in the form of requests to the departed for their prayers— dates back to very early Christian antiquity.   Our English Churchmanship is criticised by our Russian friends because—in the absence of any avowed or widespread practice of invocation—we appear to them to be lacking in any effective sense of present communion with the saints.   To what extent, if at all, are we to recognise the justice of this criticism ?   Is it in any degree true that existing prejudices against " Rome " have prevented fair consideration being given amongst us to the case for a practice which is not in itself distinctively Roman, and which, even if it were, should be judged, either way, upon its merits ?   The revival of invocation within recent years under strong official discouragement—often, it must be confessed in forms which are unwise, and from motives which are frankly reactionary—makes it impossible to evade a discussion of this issue.   There is no doubt that the practice of invocation may easily be degraded into superstition.   The mediæval period witnessed an enormous development of the cultus of the saints in all its forms, and there can be little question that in much of the *popular* piety of the Middle Ages the saints had come to take virtually the place of God.   The sixteenth-century Reformers were led to remove from the public services of the Church of England all forms of invocation, direct or indirect ; and, though there is certainly not at the present time any widespread popular demand for the reintroduction of forms

of invocation into public worship, the question is
sometimes asked whether loss, as well as gain, has
not resulted from their suppression. We seem to
have lost the sense of the Christian *family*, the
consciousness of the approach of all God's children
together to the throne of their common Father. We
declare in the Liturgy that it is " with angels and
archangels, and with all the company of heaven,"
that we laud and magnify God's glorious Name,
but do we in actual practice, as we say the words,
realise their meaning ? And may it not be that
there is a connection between our defective sense
of mystical brotherhood in the Church of Christ
with those departed, and that desolating absence of
the spirit of brotherhood and fellowship amongst
the living, which is so manifest an anomaly in
our modern Church life ? Certainly in the religion
of the Russian peasants, as described, for example,
in the works of Mr. Stephen Graham, the sense of
brotherhood between members of the Church on
earth is developed side by side with the most vivid
realisation of their fellowship in Christ with all
such as in the past were chosen vessels of God's
grace, and lights of the world in their several
generations.

The Roman Church, as is well known, draws a
hard-and-fast and (as we must needs think) a
somewhat arbitrary distinction between *canonised*
" saints," who are regarded as having already
attained to " heaven," and whose prayers it is
customary to invoke, and the faithful departed
in general, who are regarded as being in " purgatory," and for whose spiritual progress it is
customary to pray. The Eastern Church with

truer wisdom refrains from so rigid a classification, and, while reverencing the more notable " saints " of Christian history with special honour, nevertheless prays equally for *all* the faithful and requests the prayers of all.   An Eastern Christian will with equal simplicity request the prayers of his mother who has passed into the unseen world, and offer his own prayers to God on behalf of the Mother of our Lord.   What is to be our own view of this whole matter ?

It cannot be denied that the practice of invoking the prayers of the saints may easily be attended by obvious dangers.   It is difficult not to think that those who habitually invoke by name the great saints and heroes of the past to assist them by their prayers are apt to slip, almost without knowing it, into a conception of God which is less than Christian : they may come to regard Him, that is to say, as an Oriental despot surrounded by his courtiers,* in approaching whom it is desirable to have " friends at court," rather than as a Father to whom they have direct access through Christ.   The conception of particular saints as being entrusted, under God, with a kind of delegated sovereignty over particular departments of life— as where, for example, St. Antony is regarded as " the saint who helps you to find things when you have lost them,"etc.—is especially to be deprecated; and in popular Romanism there is often a kind of *badgering* of the saints which is far from edifying, and seems little calculated in actual practice to

* See, with reference to the " Sultanic " conception of God, the Rev. Harold Anson's essay on " Prayer as Understanding " in the recent volume *Concerning Prayer*, published by Messrs. Macmillan & Co., under the editorship of Canon Streeter.

intensify the conception of the Church as a mystical family, in which the departed are knit together with the living in virtue of their common sonship to God. Roman Catholic theologians, it is true, are careful to insist that the saints are to be reverenced and approached not in virtue of any merits of their own but as the vessels of God's grace : that it is Christ, as manifested in His saints, and not the saints as such, to whom reverence is due. Anglicanism has suffered greatly by leaving the empty spaces unpeopled, instead of regarding the unseen world as filled with the living presences of those whom we call " the dead." But there would seem to be in popular Catholic piety a real danger of making virtual demigods of the saints : and the traditional Anglican caution with regard to this particular matter has not a little to commend it. It may be hoped that if the practice of invocation is to be unofficially revived among us it will be the Eastern rather than the Roman model that is followed. Assuming that we are right in thinking that those who have passed into the unseen world are not kept in ignorance of the world which they have left, it is plainly not unnatural for one who has been accustomed to ask for the prayers on his behalf of some still living friend, if the friend in question is removed by death, to continue to request his prayers in the sphere where he now dwells with Christ, and to be comforted by the thought that his friend still prays for him with an ever-deepening insight into God's purposes on his behalf. There will be many, doubtless, to whom even so modified a form of invocation as this will make no appeal : but in any case, whether we do, or whether we do not, for our own part, directly *request* the saints to pray for us, we do well to realise, with what vividness we may, the truth that they *do* pray for us; to be conscious of the "cloud of witnesses"; and perhaps to say sometimes, in our own prayers to our Heavenly Father, "May the communion of Thy saints be our comfort, and the prayers of Thy saints our defence."

Those who think often of the saints do, in effect, find their example and the thought of their prayers on our behalf to be a power. They, being dead, yet speak: and they, being alive unto God, are one with us still in sacrament and prayer. It is beyond dispute that many thousands of the soldiery of France in the present war have been nerved and encouraged and made strong by the thought of one who five centuries ago (to the shame of England) was executed at Rouen by a judicial murder as brutal and as disgraceful as the execution at Brussels by the Germans of Edith Cavell; and who shall say that they were not helped also—as they themselves believed—by the actual prayers of Joan of Arc herself, who, being alive unto God, is in a true sense still the patroness of France?

And, if the communion of saints is thus a fellowship of prayer, it is equally a fellowship of *mutual* prayer. Mutuality is in truth of the essence of fellowship, and if the departed, as we believe, pray for us, it is our part, surely, to pray for them. Even earlier in Christian history than the invocation of the departed is the practice of prayer on their behalf; and many who for their own part feel

bound to hold aloof from the former practice yet
feel instinctively the rightness of the latter. It
would seem, indeed, that if we have any faith in
immortality—if we do veritably believe the departed still to exist and to be alive unto God—then
are we bound to pray on their behalf. If we are
to " give thanks always for all men," we are also
to pray for all. It is strange that any Christian
should shrink from commending unto the loving
mercy of God the souls of those whom he has loved
and lost, from asking that God would grant unto
them a place of refreshment, light, and peace, where
all sighing and sadness are vanished away, and the
light of His countenance shineth for ever and ever.
True it is that we believe that God will do, both
for them and for us, exceeding abundantly above
all that we ask or think. " Your Heavenly
Father knoweth what things ye have need of "
—and He knows what things our friends have
need of, whom we commend to His keeping—
" before ye ask Him." But our Lord uttered the
words I have quoted, not as a rationalistic objection
against prayer, but as a reason for praying. It is
precisely *because* our Father knows better than we
do, and *because* He will do more than we ask or
think, that we are encouraged to prattle out before
Him, as little children, all that is in our hearts. If
" we know not what to pray for as we ought,"
nevertheless " the Spirit helpeth our infirmities " ;
and these considerations apply as directly to
prayer for the departed as to prayer for the living.
All the rationalistic difficulties and objections
which men not uncommonly raise with regard to
prayer for the departed are in principle objections

against the practice of prayer in general. It is difficult to frame a wholly satisfactory intellectual theory of prayer; but the practice of prayer, nevertheless, lies at the very heart of all religion. We cannot in any case go wrong if we ask, on behalf of those who have passed beyond the grave and gate of death, for those things which St. Paul asked on behalf of his converts, namely, that God would grant unto them, according to the riches of His glory, to be strengthened with might by His Spirit in the inward man: that Christ may increasingly dwell in their hearts by faith: and that they, in whatever region of being they now are, may be rooted and grounded in love, and be strong to comprehend with all saints what is the breadth and length and depth and height, and to know the love of Christ which passeth knowledge, and to be filled with all the fullness of God.

It may be that our prayer is in a manner already answered ere ever it is offered. The time relationship has in any case but little bearing upon the mystery of prayer. Prejudice and pedantry are alike impotent to prevail against the instinctive impulses of Christian love; and whatever we desire or hope for those departed we are right to make known with boldness before the throne of God.

Prejudices in this particular matter are in truth rapidly dying down; many Protestant Nonconformists as well as a growing number of Anglicans are learning simply and naturally to commend to God's keeping the souls of those who have gone before them with the sign of faith, and now do rest in the sleep of peace. The plain man, who

P

approaches these things without prejudice, will
have no hesitation in the matter. Nor will those
who believe that God is a God of love be disposed
to limit their intercessions to the case of specifically
Christian dead. For we know that God is One to
Whom no prayer is ever made without hope of
mercy, and Who hath no pleasure in the death of
a sinner, but would have *all* men to be saved, and
to come to the knowledge of the truth.

XIII

FORGIVENESS

"The Forgiveness of sins."

FORGIVENESS of Sins is the first great gift which is offered to man through the Gospel of Christ. It is the first—and perhaps we might say the most important—because everything else which Christ came to bring depends upon it. Jesus Christ came to bring men into fellowship with God. Forgiveness is the first step to this fellowship, for it removes the great hindrance which stands in the way—namely, Sin. When we look into the Gospel story we find how large a place this subject of forgiveness takes. The way is prepared for our Lord by one whose message is, "Repent ye, for the Kingdom of God is at hand." Our Lord Himself when He begins to preach takes up the same message. Nor can any of the good gifts of the Kingdom be received until people are in the right frame of mind to ask forgiveness of their sins.

As our Lord's ministry continued, the importance of forgiveness seems to have been often in His mind. People pressed around Him seeking many other things, chiefly the healing of their bodies. He did not repel them, but often whilst He healed their bodies He added a further gift for the needs of their souls. In one case when a man was brought for healing, He surprised all by forgiving his sins first, as though that were the greater need (St. Mark ii. 1–12).

Moreover, by His whole manner our Lord showed that the needs of sinners were His special care. They felt strongly drawn to Him, and He was so much with them that He drew down upon Himself the anger of respectable people. He went to eat with publicans, who were social outcasts. The standing complaint against Him was, " This man receiveth sinners and eateth with them." Again, He was contemptuously spoken of as " A friend of publicans and sinners."

A remarkable instance of this occurs in St. Luke vii. 37 ff. We are told that " a woman which was a sinner " came to Him as He sat at meat. She offered Him the respectful but loving attentions of a repentant soul. The host was scandalised, but our Lord rebuked him and commended the woman. He assured her that her sins were forgiven, and sent her away in peace. Thus we see that our Lord took peculiar pains to insist that God forgives sinners, and that forgiveness is what men chiefly need.

But there are two more points that we must notice here. In the first place, no matter how grievously men have sinned, God still desires to forgive them. And He will forgive if the sinner asks Him to do so. Our Lord prayed for the soldiers who crucified Him, because hardened as they were they did not really know what they were doing (St. Luke xxiii. 34). They might come to know, and then perhaps they would be sorry. So, too, the dying robber had only to turn with all his heart to the Saviour beside him. The word of pardon came at once in reply.

In the second place, so far from God being unwilling to forgive, we are told that there is more joy in heaven over one repentant sinner than over many who do not need repentance. This special joy of God in forgiving sinners is recorded in St. Luke xv., the chapter which, perhaps, more than any other brings us to the heart of the New Testament teaching about forgiveness. God seeks the sinner, because otherwise he would be helpless. No pains are spared because the sinner is so precious. Lastly, nothing can exceed the generosity and love with which the sinner is welcomed on his return. The prodigal son hears no word of reproach when he comes back. There is nothing but gladness. The tide of Love rises and covers all the wrong that has been done. The father's only thought is to celebrate a feast of joy. " Let us eat and make merry : for this my son was dead, and is alive again ; he was lost, and is found."

The forgiveness which God offers is, therefore, a free gift. It does not depend upon any goodness or merit in us, as though we could deserve it. The worst people receive it. The publicans and harlots, we are told, sometimes go into the Kingdom of God before others. They have no qualifications ; but by that very fact, perhaps, they are more easily brought to repentance and so made fit to receive the gift. They have no pride to keep them back by suggesting that they do not need it. The fact is that the gift does not depend upon *our* character, but upon God's. God forgives sinners because He is Love. His Love has found a way of overcoming all the difficulties. He forgives in spite of our sins, not because of our deserts. It is simply His almighty power which we see here at work. It is a power which never fails; and this is found to hold good in the experience of un-numbered sinners who by God's mercy have become saints.

It is a help sometimes to look away from our-selves, and to notice what the experience of others has been. Probably all of us have met at least one person who has had the experience of forgive-ness as a quite real and unmistakable thing. We have noticed that after this experience they have no longer doubted God's Love. He has forgiven their sins, and they are now able to approach Him in a way which, as they would say, was impossible before. In the pages of the New Testament itself we find two notable instances in the Apostles St. Peter and St. Paul. One had denied his Lord, the other had persecuted Him. Yet by God's grace both were forgiven and restored. From that time onwards they never doubted what God had done, but rejoiced in His Power. The past was forgotten in the present experience.

If, then, we are prepared to accept the guidance of the Scriptures, there can be no doubt that God forgives. But we must next consider why it is that we need this forgiveness. Probably most of those who read these pages will be quite ready to acknowledge that there has been failure in their life. We don't set up to be perfect. We have done wrong sometimes; and we can hardly fail to see that our wrongdoing has been harmful. To say the least, it has been harmful to ourselves.

We are conscious that a good deal of unhappiness comes into our life through our own shortcomings. Taking it at its lowest point, if we don't make a success of life, most of us are prepared to say it is our own fault. We might have done better. By not doing better we have injured ourselves. But we cannot stop at that point. We have injured others as well as ourselves. We are not alone in the world. The failure of one always affects others in the long run. By our individual shortcomings we wrong our fellow-men. The moral weakling does not make his contribution to society as a whole. He is a kind of parasite. He is living upon the energies and the strength of character which belong to others. In some instances, we can see this very clearly. A healthy family life depends upon the good temper and the mutual helpfulness of all the members of the family. Bad temper, sloth, unkindness, will all tend to break up the family life. But if we looked a little further into this we should see that all wrongdoing spoils our common life together. Our failure, therefore, not only injures ourselves, but wrongs our fellow-men. But once again we cannot stop at this point. Conscience tells us that there is another wrong, far deeper than those first two. We have wronged God, and that is infinitely more serious.

This is the only satisfactory explanation of the other two facts. God made us to do right, and we have done wrong. We have been acting contrary to our true nature, and so, like the prodigal son, we have been walking away from the Father's love and entering a country where soon we find that nothing can really satisfy us. A want has come into our life which only God can fill. Yet we have been trying to fill it with the husks of lesser interests. It is true that we may be occupied with many things which are good and useful. But by themselves they have no power to satisfy our deepest spiritual needs. For all their worth they are little better then husks, if we have forgotten God in our pursuit of them. In wronging ourselves we have wronged God, and the wrong done to other people is a natural consequence. In leaving his father, the prodigal left his home and his brother. There is no more lonely person than the unforgiven sinner. He has estranged himself from both God and his fellow-men. The Bible tells us that we are all sinners. We have not only failed, but we have sinned. " All have sinned and come short of the glory of God."

Now the trouble is, that one of the effects of sin is to make us blind to our real condition. We don't see our danger, or see it only in part. Sin has a way of acting like a drug. It tends to bring on a state of indifference in which people don't know what is wrong, and sometimes, at last, don't care either. What we need most, then, is to be roused up, to come to ourselves. God wants to forgive, but there is danger lest we should not see it. Then we should for ever, perhaps, be the losers without knowing what we have lost. It is small wonder that some people to-day scoff at the very idea of sin, and say it is old-fashioned. They do not see that this is in itself a sign showing how great their need is.

What, then, must the sinner do ? Two things :

he must repent and believe. " Repent ye." " Believe on the Lord Jesus, and thou shalt be saved." Neither of these two things is easy. They are not, indeed, possible without God's help. The first thing the sinner needs to do, therefore, is to pray for the help of God's Holy Spirit. God is longing to forgive. He is more ready to hear than we are to pray. Yet, He cannot forgive unless we ask for forgiveness. And we cannot rightly ask for that gift until we see our need of it. Our eyes must be opened to see the state to which sin has brought us. So we must pray for light and God will assuredly give it. In answer to our prayer He will show us two things : His own love and our sinfulness. In seeing those two things in contrast, we shall begin to understand the real gulf which separates us from God. But we shall also begin to long that the gulf may be bridged. We shall want to be forgiven.

Now there are probably many souls that have gone as far as this in the way of repentance. They see how serious their sins have been. They feel the full force of separation from God. But perhaps at this point they are tempted to despair. How can such sins really be done away with ? Yet to fall into despair is fatal. Perhaps it is as dangerous as to remain indifferent. For what is it that makes people despair about their sins ? It is surely that they have been looking at one half of the truth, and have forgotten the other half. They have realised that they are sinners. But they have allowed that fact to make them blind to God's love. It is true that they have sinned, and sin can never undo itself. But the power of

God's love can undo it, and is ready to undo it as soon as they turn to Him and put their trust in His love. God's offer of forgiveness through His Son is perfectly clear. He is eager to welcome the sinner back again. If we know our sin and sincerely repent, then only one more thing is needful: "Believe on the Lord Jesus." Throw yourself upon God's mercy and trustfully ask for His forgiveness through Jesus Christ our Lord. Remember the words : "Him that cometh to Me I will in no wise cast out ". (St. John vi. 37).

We have now reached certain clear facts which any one who will can discover in the teaching of the Bible. We are all sinners. We need God's forgiveness. God is ready and anxious to forgive if we will come to Him in repentance and faith and ask for the gift.

But immediately a further question suggests itself : *How* does God forgive sins ? This question has already in part been answered in an earlier paper in this volume (No. V. *Jesus Christ and Sin*). The Atoning Sacrifice of Jesus Christ is the foundation upon which all forgiveness rests. That is the way which God's love has provided. God is able to forgive here and now because Atonement has been made, and God's righteous wrath against sin has been satisfied by this great fact. If, then, we still doubt how it can be possible for God to forgive sins, let us look to the Cross itself for the true answer to our difficulty. For there we may see the two things which we want to understand, the Love which is able to forgive and the sin which needs forgiveness. The sufferings and death of

our Saviour show us what God is like. His love
for sinners was so great that He gave up His Son
to a shameful death. On the other hand, we see
here, too, what sin is really like in all its horror
and malignity. It is always what it was then, the
shameful enemy of God's love. The meaning of
the Cross, then, is that Love has grappled with sin
and overcome it, because Love is the stronger.
There is nothing arbitrary or artificial about the
gift of pardon. Love has won it for sinners at a
terrible price. Moreover, this forgiveness does not
let us off the natural results of our past sins. The
injury which we have done to our character
remains. After forgiveness we shall still need to
be made holy. This may take long years of
struggle. Yet here, too, the love of God which has
forgiven us will triumph again if we hold fast to it
in penitence and trust.

We must now pass on to ask if there is any
further condition of receiving forgiveness. In
the New Testament we find that there is. The
Death of Christ is put first in the preaching of the
Apostles. But Baptism is always added as a
second condition. Thus St. Peter, on the Day of
Pentecost, said: "Repent ye and be baptized
every one of you, in the Name of Jesus Christ unto
the remission of your sins" (Acts ii. 38). To St.
Paul, too, at his conversion, there came the command: "Arise, and be baptized, and wash away
thy sins" (Acts xxii. 16). These examples are
typical. In the Church of the apostolic days
baptism is always the means by which forgiveness
of sins is *first* received in the Christian life. Christ's
gift of forgiveness is for those who are made

Christians through baptism as He ordained. If we put together these two facts just considered, it will help us to see how God has put forgiveness within the reach of us all. By the Atoning Sacrifice He has made it possible for all to be forgiven. In the sacrament of Baptism He has provided a way by which it is within our reach. This is of the greatest importance. If we are still unbaptized, we have only to seek the gift by being baptized, and our sins will be washed away according to the Divine promise. If, however, as is the case with most of us, we were baptized in childhood, that fact is of the greatest importance to us now that we are seeking forgiveness. For as baptized Christians we have already received pardon for our sins once. By baptism we were brought into the Church, which is the fellowship of God's forgiven people.

But how does all this bear upon our present position as sinners needing forgiveness afresh ?

In the first place, the fact that he has already received forgiveness once makes sin in a Christian a very serious matter. For at the time of his baptism he, or his godparents on his behalf, made a solemn promise that he would renounce all sin. A person who has not been baptized has given no such undertaking. St. John tells us that in the normal life of the Christian, sin has no proper place at all (1 St. John v. 18). Sin in the Christian is a contradiction in the deepest sense. It contradicts his whole profession. For he is under a special obligation to God ; and he is also bound to his fellow-Christians by a peculiarly intimate tie, for they are fellow-members in one Body united in

Christ. Both of these two great bonds—the bond with God and the bond with his fellow-Christians —are deeply violated by sin. The Church which we have entered by baptism has the great responsibility of bringing home these facts to us and keeping them constantly before our minds.

That is why the Prayer Book of the Church of England has such a great deal to say about sin to those who use it. The three regular services of the Church are full of warnings and advice on the subject. Both Morning and Evening Prayer begin in this way. They call us to confess our sins before we approach God in common worship. Though children of God we are all sinners who have not kept our baptismal garments white. It is, therefore, fitting that we should make a common acknowledgment of this fact when we seek to enter God's Presence together. The same principle holds good still more strongly when we come to the service of Holy Communion. In that service those that come to receive the Holy Communion are urged in still sterner words to make a true repentance. There, too, they unite in acknowledging that the burden of their sins is intolerable, and in seeking forgiveness.

But the Church does not only warn us. It is also part of her duty to give us the assurance of forgiveness when we have confessed our sins. It was through the ministry of the Church that we received the first and greatest gift of forgiveness in Holy Baptism. Nothing could be more natural, then, than that we should look to the Church for help, when we are once more in need of forgiveness. So the confession which the Prayer Book puts into our mouths is answered by the absolution spoken by the mouth of the priest. Each of the General Confessions already mentioned is followed in the Prayer Book services by a form of Absolution. In all this nothing is said or done which in any way deprives us of our right and privilege as Christians. As members of Christ we have been brought into the way of forgiveness once and for all. The Christian has always access to God by right of his baptism. He can seek forgiveness directly and privately if he will; and in answer to his faith, God will renew the baptismal gift if he truly repent. Yet, seeing that sin in a Christian is such a very grievous thing, he may well feel that this private way is not all that he needs. There is the blinding power of sin, for example. Perhaps he has deceived himself into a false security, so that his repentance is quite inadequate. Or, again, he may be in danger of despair and in urgent need of some reassurance. Now, it is exactly to meet such needs that Absolution is given in the Church. It comes in not to hinder, but to help. After Confession, which should deepen the sense of sin, there follows Absolution to give to the uncertain heart of the sinner the confident assurance of God's forgiveness.

This is a general principle which may obviously be applied in a variety of different ways. The General Confession of the congregation is naturally answered by a General Absolution. We have two such forms of Absolution in the Prayer Book. At Morning and Evening Prayer the priest makes a solemn declaration that God does forgive. This is clearly intended to help the people to claim God's forgiveness then and there. In the service of Holy Communion a step further is taken. Here the priest actually prays that God will pardon those who are present. "Almighty God . . . pardon and deliver you from all your sins." This is a prayer spoken in the name of the Church, and may be regarded as *conveying* forgiveness to those present who dispose themselves so to receive it.

Thus far Confession and Absolution are both in general terms. They help because they are done in common and in public in the presence of both God and the Church. But they only apply in a general way. There is no special mention of particular sins. The Prayer Book, however, takes us a stage further in two places. The first of these is in the long exhortation which follows immediately after the prayer for the Church Militant, near the middle of the service of Holy Communion. This exhortation stands at the threshold of the most solemn part of the service. It is a public warning which the priest is required to read to those who intend shortly to come to Holy Communion. It is a warning the chief purpose of which is to remind us of the danger of being unworthy communicants. If sin is a serious thing in the Christian under all circumstances, it becomes most serious when he is drawing near to the Altar to receive the Body and Blood of Christ. We are, therefore, here told of the great danger of being communicants without taking pains to put away our sins. Next the exhortation goes on to show us the best way to do this. We are to examine ourselves carefully in the light of God's revealed law. We are to ask ourselves questions about our life to see where we have gone wrong. We must do this solemnly and prayerfully as in God's presence. We are to seek for true sorrow for sin, and to be ready to set right any wrong which we may have done to our neighbours. This last point is specially important. We cannot hope for forgiveness if we do not try to be in love and charity with our neighbours. We must be ready to forgive them their sins against us also, as our Lord taught us. We must look upon all our fellow-Christians as though they were our Lord Himself in this respect. For they are in Him; and we cannot sincerely seek His love without wishing to be at one with them also. We must, then, make this real and full repentance with sorrow and willingness to amend our lives at all points. Unless we do that (and nothing short of that will do) Holy Communion will do us more harm than good.

These facts have too often kept away from Communion many who should have come. They have rightly felt that they could not be sure about their repentance. The pity is that such people have not taken to heart the closing portion of this exhortation, which so exactly meets their need. " And because it is requisite that no man should come to the Holy Communion, but *with a full trust in God's mercy, and with a quiet conscience;* therefore, if there be any of you who by this means cannot quiet his own conscience herein, but requireth further comfort or counsel, let him come to me, or to some other discreet and learned Minister of God's Word, and open his grief; that by the ministry of God's holy Word he may receive the benefit of absolution, together with ghostly counsel and advice, to the quieting of his conscience, and avoiding of all scruple and doubtfulness."

Warning is rightly followed by advice. The advice is, that where trust falters and conscience is unquiet a special confession should be made privately to the priest.* The confession must in this case make a particular mention of sins. The reason for this is clear. The priest is asked to give a special assurance of forgiveness to a particular individual. He cannot do this unless he knows the sins of which conscience accuses the individual in question. The sinner comes to him as to a specially appointed and specially qualified officer of the Church. He is asked to judge the case for the Church. He is helped in this by the fact that he has received authority from the Church to "remit" sins at the time of his Ordination. He has also received the gift of the Holy Spirit to enable him to use this power aright (see the service for the Ordering of Priests). Moreover, this authority in turn is derived from our Lord Himself, Who committed it to His Church (St. John xx. 21–23). The confession then must make detailed mention of all the sins which render the conscience "unquiet"; and when this is done the priest has power to give absolution. He gives it only after deciding in his own mind by God's help that repentance is real and complete. If he doubts this he may be justified in withholding absolution until he is sure that the penitent is in earnest. Under these conditions the fullest measure

* "Discreet and learned minister" was a term formerly applied to priests specially fitted for this work.

Q

of assurance possible on earth can be reached by the perplexed conscience.

The Prayer Book gives us one more piece of guidance about the use of this "sacramental" form of Confession and Absolution. It is to be found in the Office for the Visitation of the Sick. There the priest is told to " move " the sick person " to make a special confession of his sins, if he feels his conscience troubled with any weighty matter." There follows the direct form of absolution which is in general use on all such occasions. " I absolve thee from all thy sins in the Name of the Father and of the Son and of the Holy Ghost." Sin before communion is serious. Sin, in view of the possibility of death, is perhaps a more pressing burden still. Those, then, who are in danger of dying unforgiven are to be urged to " make their confession " to the priest. This is a special case. The general principle of the Church of England is that her children shall use this means of grace of their own free will. The language of the Prayer Book, however, suggests that in many cases it will not only be desirable and helpful when voluntarily sought. There will be many other people whose case is as pressing as that of the sick man. Yet through indifference or for some other reason they will have held back. Church-people will, therefore, expect to find their clergy from time to time " moving " them to " make their confessions." This will not necessarily mean that their liberty is being infringed upon. The responsibility of decision will still rest with the individual, unless his sins be so open and grievous that for his soul's sake he must be warned to abstain from Communion. It is obvious that there must be some limits to liberty in any society. The Church has the power to expel in extreme cases. But apart from such extreme cases, the Church calls upon us to make our confession to a priest only in obedience to conscience.

If we are given this liberty of conscience, however, no man can lightly pass by the warnings we have been considering. Moreover, the blessing to be received through confession is so great that we cannot afford to neglect it. People who go to confession find that they obtain through it both the joy of pardon and new strength to overcome their sins. Perhaps the majority of Christians would be vastly more secure in their hold upon the way of salvation if they had learned to value this great means of forgiveness. However that may be, surely the National Mission summons all of us to face the question afresh. May not this strong assurance of absolution be something which will satisfy our soul's need ?

XIV

THE LIFE AFTER DEATH

"The Resurrection of the body, and the life everlasting."

THE belief in some sort of personal immortality is as old and as widely diffused as any belief in the world. The most primitive forms of ancient religion of which we have any knowledge made much of attempts to propitiate the ghosts of the departed. And at the present day the most backward races of mankind seem to be agreed in believing that the spirits of their ancestors are capable of affecting their lives for good or evil.

It is possible that dreams have had something to do with prompting this belief in the first instance. However this may be, the fact remains that the vast majority of mankind have always believed that death is not absolute annihilation. And as mankind has advanced in civilization the belief has tended, upon the whole, to become stronger and more definite. Because as the struggle to procure the barest necessities of physical life becomes less insistent, man becomes increasingly conscious that he is a spiritual being. And as this consciousness increases he feels more and more strongly that the deepest part of him, his true and essential nature, cannot attain its full development under the conditions of life upon earth. They hamper it, and the time allotted—a century at the very most—is insufficient. He is conscious of such large possibilities within himself that he feels that they must at some time in the future have a larger scope than earth can afford. Human life means so much already that it must be going to mean even more.

The two most highly civilized nations of the ancient world—the Egyptians and the Persians—held a very full, clear and definite belief in the immortality of the human soul : in their eyes it seems to have been self-evident. The Greeks and Romans were less positive upon the point, but the balance of opinion among them was decidedly in favour of personal survival. The Hebrews seem to have had less conception of any life beyond the grave than almost any prominent nation of antiquity. Their minds were, perhaps, of too unspeculative a cast to be strongly attracted to the idea. It may have seemed to them to be too remote and abstract to be of much interest. They were clear that God is to be served in this life. Beyond that they hardly cared to look. Hezekiah could even speak of death as separation from God and as an end to all opportunity of serving Him. " *For the grave cannot praise Thee, death cannot celebrate Thee ; they that go down into the pit cannot hope for Thy truth. The living, the living, he shall praise Thee, as I do this day ; the father to the children shall make known Thy truth* " (Isaiah xxxviii. 18, 19). The passages of the Bible prior to the New Testament which speak quite clearly and definitely of life after death are not earlier than the second century B.C. (Daniel xii. 2, 3 ;

Wisdom iii. 1–8 ; v. 15, 16 ; 2 Maccabees xii. 43–45).
Among the Jews of Palestine in our Lord's time
belief in a future life was still a matter of opinion.
It was possible to count as an orthodox Jew and
yet deny it altogether. It was one of the points
of difference between the Pharisees and Sadducees.
St. Paul turned this to account when he was
brought before a court containing representatives
of both parties. "*But when Paul perceived that
the one part were Sadducees, and the other Pharisees,
he cried out in the Council, ' Men and brethren, I am
a Pharisee, the son of a Pharisee : of the hope and
resurrection of the dead I am called in question.' And
when he had so said there arose a dissension between
the Pharisees and the Sadducees, and the multitude
was divided. For the Sadducees say that there is no
resurrection, neither angel nor spirit : but the
Pharisees confess both*" (Acts xxiii. 6–8).

In this respect, then, as in many others, the
Christian Gospel did not create an entirely new
conception. It took an idea—namely, that death
is not absolute annihilation—with which, in varying
forms, the world as a whole was already more
or less familiar. It expanded enormously what it
took, and invested it with a definiteness and
certainty which it could not otherwise have
possessed. Thus the Christian Church has been
able to make more of the life to come than any
other religion can feel justified in doing. The
Resurrection of the Dead has always stood in the
forefront of Christian preaching and always must.
To a heathen the hope of a life after death cannot
be more than an adjunct to his creed, and it is
open to him to entertain doubts about it. To the

Christian it is the foundation upon which the whole structure of our belief is carried. No one who believes that death is the inevitable end of our personal consciousness can be a Christian at all in any sense. And the conviction upon which we build is much larger than the hope of any other creed.

This transformation of a hope, which could never be quite free from uncertainty, into an overwhelming conviction was effected by the fact in which the Church has always believed—namely, that Jesus Christ died and was buried, and that afterwards He showed Himself to His followers to be alive by many infallible proofs. These demonstrations began upon the third day after His death and were continued at intervals during a period of some forty days. The accounts which we have of them are not complete, and cannot be exactly harmonized. But they all testify to the one outstanding and marvellous fact—that He Who had been certainly dead was now as certainly alive.

It would be out of place to attempt here any summary of the arguments which lead us to believe that the Resurrection narratives in the four Gospels are what they profess to be—namely, true history written within the lifetime of men who had witnessed the events which they describe. The chain of reasoning is a long and intricate one, and its strength cannot be fully appreciated except by those who have had some experience in dealing with problems of historical and literary criticisms. The simplest and strongest argument for the Resurrection of our Lord is the existence of the

Christian Church to-day. That is an undoubted fact. But how did the Church come into being ?

For, apart from the Resurrection, the life of Jesus Christ was, upon the showing of His own followers, a complete failure. He did not do what they had expected. He did not restore again the kingdom to Israel. Whatever supernatural powers He may have seemed to possess failed Him at the moment when He had most need of them. He proved to be powerless in the hands of His enemies and they put Him to a very shameful death. The Crucifixion was a terrible catastrophe, and His followers buried all their hopes in the tomb which Joseph lent to receive His Body.

But something changed all this failure into triumph. Otherwise there would be no Christian Church in the world now. How could there be ? What could have been sufficient to bring about the change ? Something so wonderful as to be all but incredible was needed to put new heart and hope into the dispirited, beaten men which our Lord's disciples were on the evening of the first Good Friday. The Church has never doubted the cause of the change. The Apostles became new men with a Gospel to preach worth more than all the world beside, because they knew that after His death and burial they had seen Him again alive. If we do not accept that explanation we must offer another, which must be adequate. And Christians believe that none can be found. Certainly none has been found yet.

It is difficult to believe in the Resurrection of our Lord. But when we consider what the course of history has undoubtedly been we are plunged into more and worse difficulties if we deny it.

But when a Christian speaks of the life to come he has in view something more than the old doctrine of the immortality of the soul. We believe in the Resurrection of the Body, and this particular article of our Faith seems to be a point of peculiar difficulty to many thoughtful people at the present day. Immortality of the soul they are ready and anxious to believe. But the Resurrection of the Body is in their eyes an antiquated conception which is now seen to be absurd and impossible.

The Christian belief has often been interpreted in a very materialistic fashion, with results which may fairly be described as "impossible" and "absurd." For those who hold such interpretations are faced with a real difficulty when they are asked such questions as, "What happens to a man whose body has been eaten by a tiger?" or "In view of the fact that our bodies are completely renewed every seven years, which of the various bodies which we have possessed will be the one to rise again?" The Church has never endorsed any interpretation which would make such difficulties real. It is not bound by any misconstruction of its words which may have gained currency. Almost all Christian beliefs are liable to be interpreted wrongly because they are so wide and deep that it is not easy to grasp more than a small fraction of their true content.

When we say in the Creed, "I believe in the Resurrection of *the Body*," what do we really mean?

Briefly, we mean that ultimately we shall lose nothing by death.

The Body is at present a real part of us. It is the indispensable medium of our self-expression. We cannot think without a brain, or speak without tongue, lips and breath, or act without hands and feet. A disembodied spirit is less than a whole man. If only a part of us is to survive death our immortality is only partial. Partial immortality is indeed something ; but if only part of us is to survive there can be nothing which can be considered a conquest of death. Death takes a very heavy and permanent toll of us. All that can be said is that it does not take quite everything.

But the Christian belief is that, as we say in the Collect for Easter Sunday, Christ *overcame death ;* or, in the language of St. Paul, " *Death hath no more dominion over Him* " (Romans vi. 9). And, further, that Christ's conquest of death is not an eternally isolated phenomenon, but an anticipation of the final destiny of our race. We, too, are destined ultimately to *overcome* death in like manner.

This is a very much larger and more difficult conception than the old belief in the immortality of the soul. We could not have reached it by any process of unaided reasoning. But we believe that it has been forced upon us by facts. The Church has been led to formulate it by the narratives of the appearances of the Risen Lord.

Unless we are to dismiss the Resurrection narratives as works of fiction we must recognize that our Lord was—as we may say—at pains to convince His followers that He was not a disembodied spirit. It was natural that they should think that He was ; but He made it plain that He was not.

" *And as they thus spake, Jesus Himself stood in the midst of them, and saith unto them, Peace be unto you. But they were terrified and affrighted, and supposed that they had seen a spirit. And He said unto them, Why are ye troubled ? and why do thoughts arise in your hearts ? Behold My hands and My feet, that it is I Myself : handle Me, and see ; for a spirit hath not flesh and bones, as ye see Me have. And when He had thus spoken, He shewed them His hands and His feet. And while they yet believed not for joy, and wondered, He said unto them, Have ye here any meat ? And they gave Him a piece of a broiled fish and of an honeycomb. And He took it, and did eat before them* "* (St. Luke xxiv. 36–43).* Compare also St. John xx. 27 and xxi. 13.

If the narratives of St. Luke and St. John be true history, the Being who appeared to His followers was a Man, not a Ghost : albeit He was not exactly as He had been before.

But our evidence for the point is not confined to the Gospels. St. Paul makes a further contribution to the belief, and the importance of his testimony often seems to be overlooked. Upon what did St. Paul base his doctrine of the Spiritual Body ? In the First Epistle to the Corinthians (xv. 35–55)—the passage is too long to be quoted in full here—he develops a doctrine of a " *Spiritual Body* " and its relation to what he calls the " *Natural Body.*"

The doctrine is not easy to understand, and

the illustrations which he quotes from the physical world do not make it very much clearer. I imagine that most readers of the Bible have felt the obscurity of the passage : I venture to think that St. Paul did not understand it perfectly himself, because it is a matter necessarily beyond our present grasp. I believe he would have been much more at ease if he had not felt obliged to speak of a "Spiritual Body" and could have launched into a rhapsody upon the Immortality of the Soul. But for some reason he did not do so. Instead he involved himself in what might be regarded as a nearly unintelligible and needlessly complicated theory. Now it is absurd to say that a Jew of the Dispersion like St. Paul would have known nothing of the theories of the immortality of the soul current in the Greek-speaking world. It cannot be maintained that he could not conceive any life after death except in some sort of body. He could have written of the immortality of the soul if he had wished. But he elected to write of something different. I believe he knew that belief in the immortality of the soul is less than the whole truth. As a theory it was not large enough to cover what he knew he had seen. He had seen Christ and had heard Him speak on the road outside Damascus : and he knew that what he had seen was not merely a spirit. The Person whom he had met was something more than that. But exactly what He was St. Paul could not say. He used the expression " *Spiritual Body* " as the nearest approach possible for human thought and speech. He ranged the physical world for such analogies to it as he could find.

From the nature of the case his search was not entirely successful; as he himself was doubtless well aware.

The evidence of the New Testament along two quite independent lines—the narratives of the Evangelists and the teaching of St. Paul—is overwhelmingly in favour of the belief which the Church has enshrined in the Apostles' Creed—namely, that as our Lord was after His Resurrection more than a disembodied spirit, so we shall ultimately possess "spiritual" or "resurrection bodies." What will be their precise relationship to the bodies in which we are living now we cannot say. Nor does the point really concern us. The point which does concern us is that we shall ultimately have lost nothing by death.

Now the Christian belief becomes impossible upon one hypothesis only. That is, if we hold that Matter and Spirit are two entities eternally distinct and eternally at war with one another. That is very commonly assumed. But it is only an assumption. It seems to have been very widely assumed throughout the East for more than two thousand years. It generally includes the view that Matter in all its forms is inherently and essentially evil. The redemption for which an Oriental looks—especially in Buddhism—is primarily from Matter. But Christianity traverses this theory directly. We affirm that Matter, having been created by God, can only be evil incidentally: in as far as we have elected to make it so. And therefore we look for redemption not from Matter but from Sin. Thus there is a Christian doctrine of things material as well as of things spiritual. Matter and Spirit do seem to us at present to be entirely distinct, and we know that they are often at war. The New Testament dwells continually upon the strife between them. But it is not true that they are always at war. They are conjoined in each one of us at present, and up to a point they are allies. The Spirit makes use of the Body to give effect to its motions. It cannot give effect to them without it. And up to a point it finds the Body a useful and willing servant. Of course, there comes a point at which the Body fails and becomes a drag and a hindrance. The Spirit is constantly impeded by the inability of the Body to endure more than a certain amount of fatigue, or to transport itself from place to place at more than a certain speed. The two are at present mutually dependent; but the connection is not by any means—as the Oriental holds—wholly to the detriment of the Spirit. The Body could not live without the Spirit: the Spirit would be deprived of the power of self-expression without the Body.

The antagonism between Matter and Spirit is in many ways very real at present. But are we justified in assuming that it is real in the sense that it must be eternally valid ?

To take an illustration. The words "up" and "down" indicate a distinction which is real for all practical purposes here and now and cannot be ignored. But we know that we should only have to proceed a certain distance into space to deprive them of all meaning. There is neither "up" nor "down" in the interstellar void.

We may even go a step farther and point out that if " up " and " down " always meant exactly what we generally use them to mean, the people in Australia would be head downwards. Probably most children have at one time been unable to understand why they are not. The conclusion that because the earth is a ball the people upon the other side of it must be head downwards is irrefragable if we limit our ideas sufficiently at the beginning of the argument. It is a simple illustration of the fallacies into which we are sure to fall if we press unduly terms which we commonly use as a matter of practical convenience. We may easily read into them a wider and more permanent meaning than they can really possess.

I believe it is possible to exaggerate the antagonism between Matter and Spirit. It is real and vital now, but not necessarily eternal. It is possible to conceive a state of existence in which even this, the deepest of all existing discords, has been resolved and the two are perfectly harmonized. And would not that be the most perfect existence of which we can form any picture ? And if Matter can be perfectly purified and made absolutely one with Spirit, then Matter does not lie outside the Divine scheme of Redemption. The *restoration of all things* is not merely a phrase. It does really include all things.

The belief that this is possible does cover what we are told of our Lord after the Resurrection. His Body could be seen and handled, because it was a real Body. He could eat before His disciples. But His Body was not as ours are. It was not subject to the law of gravity, as our spirits are not. It could appear and disappear at will, because it was wholly and absolutely under the dominion of His Spirit. He had, indeed, conquered death in that He had brought His Body through death ; to be more perfectly in harmony with His Spirit and, therefore, a more perfect instrument of His Will than it had ever been before. His followers saw realized in Him the perfection of human nature which is the ultimate goal of our life. But for us it is still in the future.

We believe that we may win to this perfection. But we do not expect to attain it immediately after death. The New Testament tells us very little about the life to come. It teaches that there is such a life, and that in it men will be rewarded or punished according as they have lived upon earth. It also teaches plainly that the final separation between good and bad is not until the Last Judgment. Character does not reach its final stage until then. We have no ground for saying that any one " goes straight to heaven " immediately after death. But of the conditions of the future life it says nothing except in metaphorical language which is not meant to be taken literally.

We do not know in what condition those who have departed before us are now, but we may believe that they are conscious, and that they are in a state of conscious progress. Christian common sense suggests that no mortal can be at the moment of his death all, or nearly all, that God intends him to become. He is still stained with many sins. But we may believe that if he has striven earnestly to conquer his sins during this life he will continue to travel the same path, becoming conformed more and more closely to the likeness of Christ, between death and judgment. But if he has not tried to overcome his sins during this life we are not justified in assuming that he will desire to do so after death. There is no ground for thinking that death changes the direction of the will. The Bible lends no support to the idea that if opportunities for repentance and amendment of life are deliberately ignored on earth they will be renewed and grasped elsewhere. We ought rather to think of death as an emancipation of the will. After death our will will no longer be subject to many of the restrictions which are imposed upon it by the conditions of life here. We shall, therefore, be able to travel more rapidly along the path which we have already elected to tread in this life—either towards God or away from Him. It will be possible for us to rise higher or to sink lower than we could have done when on earth. But we have no reason to suppose that death in itself will be an ennobling influence.

It may be that every human soul will not live eternally. Our Lord has warned us that if we deliberately confound good and evil in this life we may reach a point at which we can no longer distinguish between them. And if we really cannot tell good from evil all hope or possibility of repentance has plainly been destroyed—by our own act. Then we are *in the grip of an eternal sin* for which there can be no forgiveness (St. Mark iii. 22–30).

And it may be that as God is the only source of all life, the soul which persists in sin until it has ceased to have anything in common with Him, until it has deliberately thrown away the power of ever having anything in common with Him, will cease to exist. Its personal consciousness will be extinguished. We may regard such a view as intrinsically probable, and may hold that it is in accordance with our Lord's teaching. Such phrases as "*where their worm dieth not, and the fire is not quenched*" (St. Mark ix. 44), look to the valley of Hinnom where the refuse of Jerusalem was destroyed. But no living thing was ever brought there. To those who heard them the words would not have suggested unending torment, but utter destruction.

But, of course, any conclusion which we may adopt upon this point cannot be more than a matter of opinion. The Church Universal has pronounced no judgment upon it.

The Life Everlasting is not perhaps a particularly felicitous phrase. *The Life of the world to come* or *Eternal Life* are preferable. For *everlasting life* does suggest something smaller than the Christian hope. It does not imply more than a mere prolongation of life through unending cycles of time. It is probably understood by many people to mean no more than that. But this view is not in keeping with our Lord's teaching. "*And this is Life Eternal, that they might know Thee the only true God, and Jesus Christ, whom Thou hast sent*" (St. John xvii. 3. Compare also St. John vi. 54 and 1 St. John iii. 14).

The difference between *life eternal* and what we may call for convenience sake *ordinary life* is not only in duration. It is in quality also. Eternal

life is life which has risen to a new level where
death can have no more power. Its quality is
the secret of its duration. It has not merely
worsted death in a struggle on what we may call
death's own ground. It has soared to heights
where death is not.

That is why the New Testament does not speak
of Eternal Life as something which lies wholly in
the future. It begins here and now. It is won—
though not in its fullest form—or lost during the
years which we spend upon earth. A Christian
does not look simply for unending prolongation
of life as we know it now. If he did, he might well
shrink from the prospect.

Our belief is that human life, in the fullness of
our whole nature, can, without ceasing to be human,
be raised to levels far above any known to us now.
Upon those levels death is no more: not because
it has been evaded, but because it has been met
and conquered. We can take the first few steps
toward those heights now. We can begin to live
eternally in this present life: that is—begin to
lead a life of the quality which will make the
defeat of death possible. And we believe that as
human life rises towards the level of the Divine
Life it experiences increasingly a happiness beyond
anything which we can now imagine. An earnest
of our happiness has been revealed to us in the
lives of the Saints, and in a smaller measure is
not perhaps altogether outside our own personal
experience. But however vivid and intense such
happiness may be now, it can be but a shadow of
the full and ultimate reality.

To sum up :

Man's consciousness of himself as a spiritual being has always forbidden him to believe that he is annihilated in the death of his body. But though the hope of personal survival has been strong apart from the Christian Gospel, the Christian Gospel alone can transform it into more than a hope.

We cannot explain away the stories of the Resurrection of our Lord. If we accept them as true, they make the undoubted course of subsequent history intelligible as nothing else can. And the Resurrection of Christ has changed the hope of personal survival into a certainty upon which we may count. At the same time it has expanded our ideas as to what personal immortality really means. For it has shown us that we shall ultimately be more than disembodied spirits. Our whole nature will triumph over death. The best for which men had dared to hope before was that a part of us would survive death.

We cannot speak positively as to the nature of the glorified body which we shall come to possess, because it is altogether outside our present experience. But we believe that it will be a real body : real as that in which the Risen Lord was seen by His disciples. Further than that we have no need to wish to go. The resurrection of the body can only be deemed impossible by those who assume that the present antagonism between Matter and Spirit is eternal. The Church has always refused to admit the common view—which would make the antagonism eternal—that Matter is essentially and inherently evil.

It is possible that one final outcome of our Lord's

Ministry of Reconciliation—already accomplished
in His own Person—will be the resolution of even
this most deep and ancient discord. Spirit and
Matter may be made perfectly one.

The life which we shall then lead will be Eternal : that is of a quality different from the life
which we lead now. It will not be merely life
unendingly prolonged despite death, but life which
has passed through the grave to a level which
death cannot reach. We can begin to live the
kind of life which will achieve this here and now.

The prospect before us is larger and nobler
than anything which we could have imagined for
ourselves. Like almost everything which the
Gospel offers, it is almost beyond belief. Our
poor faculties are constantly tempted to exclaim :
" It is too good to be true."

The Christian Gospel would be too good to be
true, it could be but a beautiful fancy, were it not
for a certain Life which was actually lived before
the eyes of men. That Life cannot be explained
away, and in it the overwhelming Christian claim
and the glorious Christian hope have a foundation
which cannot be shaken.

BIBLIOGRAPHY

[Books suitable for elementary study are marked with an asterisk *]

So far as possible, the date of first publication is given in each case, and the price stated is the lowest at which the book can be procured.

I

FAITH

*H. S. Holland, Art. *Faith* in *Lux Mundi.* Murray. 2s. 6d. 1889.

J. H. Newman, *A Grammar of Assent.* Longmans. 3s. 6d. 1870.

A. J. Balfour, *The Foundations of Belief.* Longmans. 5s. 1895.

A. J. Balfour, *Theism and Humanism.* Hodder & Stoughton. 10s. 6d. 1915.

J. R. Illingworth, *Reason and Revelation.* Macmillan. 6d. 1902.

A. Chandler, *Faith and Experience.* Methuen. 3s. 6d. 1911.

W. R. Inge, *Faith and its Psychology.* Duckworth. 2s. 6d. 1909.

W. Spens, *Belief and Practice,* cc. I.–V. Longmans. 6s. 1915.

Margaret Benson, *The Venture of Rational Faith.* Macmillan. 6s. 1908.

The Works of Bishop Butler : Vol. II. *The Analogy,* ed. J. H. Bernard. Macmillan. 4s. 6d. 1900.

*B. F. Westcott, *The Historic Faith.* Macmillan. 6d. 1883.

*W. Temple, *The Faith and Modern Thought.* Macmillan. 1s. 1910.

W. Temple, *Mens Creatrix.* Macmillan. 7s. 6d. 1917.

II

GOD

*A. B. Davidson, Art. *God* in Hastings' *Dictionary of the Bible,* Vol. II., pp. 196–205. T. & T. Clark.

*A. L. Moore, Art. *The Christian Doctrine of God*, in *Lux Mundi*. Murray. 2s. 6d. 1889.

W. N. Clarke, *The Christian Doctrine of God*. T. & T. Clark. 10s. 6d. 1909.

*J. R. Illingworth, *Personality, Human and Divine*. Macmillan. 6d. 1894.

H. Rashdall, Art. *The Ultimate Basis of Theism*, in *Contentio Veritatis*. Murray. 2s. 6d. 1902.

G. J. Romanes, *Thoughts on Religion*. Longmans. 6d. 1895.

*C. C. J. Webb, *Problems in the Relations of God and Man*. Nisbet. 7s. 6d. 1911.

F. B. Jevons, *The Idea of God in Early Religions*. Camb. Univ. Press. 1s. 3d. 1910.

F. J. Hall, *The Being and Attributes of God*. Longmans. 6s. 1909.

H. M. Gwatkin, *The Knowledge of God*, 2 vols. T. & T. Clark. 12s. 1906.

C. F. D'Arcy, *God and Freedom in Human Experience*. Arnold. 10s. 6d. 1915.

A. C. Fraser, *The Philosophy of Theism*. Blackwood. 6s. 6d. 1895–6.

For this and following sections, see the relevant passages in the following dogmatic treatises :—

H. L. Martensen, *Christian Dogmatics*. T. & T. Clark. 10s. 1878.

*T. B. Strong, *A Manual of Theology*. Black. 5s. 1892.

A. J. Mason, *The Faith of the Gospel*. Longmans. 3s. 1888.

H. C. G. Moule, *Outlines of Christian Doctrine*. Hodder & Stoughton. 2s. 6d. 1889.

D. Stone, *Outlines of Christian Dogma*. Longmans. 7s. 6d. 1900.

J. Orr, *The Christian View of God and the World*. Hodder & Stoughton. 10s. 6d. 1893.

O. C. Quick, *Essays in Orthodoxy*. Macmillan. 6s. 1916.

Also the following works on the Creeds :—

*E. C. S. Gibson, *The Three Creeds*. Longmans. 4s. 1908.

A. E. Burn, *The Apostles' Creed, The Nicene Creed, The Athanasian Creed*. Rivington. 1s. 3d. each, or in one vol. 3s. 9d. 1907, 1909, 1912.

H. B. Swete, *The Apostles' Creed.* Camb. Univ. Press. 3s. 1908.

T. Zahn, *The Articles of the Apostles' Creed.* Eng. tr. Hodder & Stoughton. 5s. 1899.

III

THE MEANING OF THE INCARNATION

*C. Gore, *The Incarnation of the Son of God.* Murray. 2s. 6d. 1891.

H. R. Mackintosh, *The Person of Jesus Christ.* T. & T. Clark. 10s. 6d. 1912.

R. L. Ottley, *The Doctrine of the Incarnation.* Methuen. 12s. 6d. 1896. Second edit. 1902.

E. H. Gifford, *The Incarnation:* a Study of Phil. II. 5-11. Longmans. 1s. 1879.

H. V. S. Eck, *The Incarnation.* Longmans. 5s. 1901.

H. M. Relton, *A Study in Christology.* S.P.C.K. 6s. 1916.

F. Weston, *The One Christ.* Longmans. 5s. 1907.

W. R. Inge, Art. *The Person of Christ,* in *Contentio Veritatis.* Murray. 2s. 6d. 1902.

P. T. Forsyth, *The Person and Place of Jesus Christ.* Hodder & Stoughton. 7s. 6d. 1909.

A. J. Mason, *The Chalcedonian Doctrine of the Incarnation.* S.P.C.K. 6d. 1913.

St. Athanasius, *De Incarnatione,* text and translation, Ed. A. Robertson, 2 vols. D. Nutt. 3s. each. 1882-4.

*P. J. Carnegie Simpson, *The Fact of Christ.* Hodder & Stoughton. 1s. 1901.

C. F. Nolloth, *The Person of our Lord and Recent Thought.* Macmillan. 6s. 1908.

*J. Denney, *Jesus and the Gospel.* Hodder & Stoughton. 10s. 6d. 1908.

J. Armitage Robinson, *Some Thoughts on the Incarnation.* Longmans. 6d. 1905.

O. C. Quick, *Modern Philosophy and the Incarnation.* S.P.C.K. 6d. 1915.

IV

JESUS CHRIST AND HISTORY

*W. Sanday, *Outlines of the Life of Christ.* T. & T. Clark. 5s. 1905.

*R. W. Dale, *The Living Christ and the Four Gospels.* Hodder & Stoughton. 6s. 1890.

P. Batiffol, *The Credibility of the Gospel.* Eng. tr. Longmans. 4s. 6d. 1912.

J. Orr, *The Virgin Birth of Christ.* Hodder & Stoughton. 2s. 1907.

G. H. Box, *The Virgin Birth of Jesus.* Pitman. 5s. 1916.

*A. C. Headlam, *The Miracles of the New Testament.* Murray. 6s. 1914.

C. F. D'Arcy, *Christianity and the Supernatural.* Longmans. 1s. 1909.

J. R. Illingworth, *The Gospel Miracles.* Macmillan. 4s. 6d. 1915.

F. C. Burkitt, *The Earliest Sources for the Life of Jesus.* Constable. 1s. 1910.

*T. R. Glover, *The Jesus of History.* Student Christian Movement. 3s. 6d. 1917.

W. P. DuBose, *The Gospel in the Gospels.* Longmans. 5s. 1906.

R. J. Knowling, *The Testimony of St. Paul to Christ viewed in some of its Aspects.* Hodder & Stoughton. 10s. 6d. 1905.

A. S. Peake, *A Critical Introduction to the New Testament.* Duckworth. 2s. 6d. 1909.

V

JESUS CHRIST AND SIN

St. Anselm, *Cur Deus Homo?* D. Nutt. 1s. 6d.

R. W. Dale, *The Atonement.* Hodder & Stoughton. 6s. 1875.

R. C. Moberly, *Atonement and Personality.* Murray. 6s. 1901.

J. M'Leod Campbell, *The Nature of the Atonement.* Macmillan. 10s. 6d.

J. Scott Lidgett, *The Spiritual Principle of the Atonement.* Kelly. 5s. 1897.

*J. Denney, *The Death of Christ,* and *The Atonement and the Modern Mind.* Hodder & Stoughton. One Vol. 6s. 1903.

P. T. Forsyth, *The Cruciality of the Cross.* Hodder & Stoughton. 5s. 1909.

P. T. Forsyth, *The Work of Christ.* Hodder & Stoughton. 5s. 1910.

H. N. Oxenham, *The Catholic Doctrine of the Atonement.* W. H. Allen. 10s. 6d. 1865.

J. G. Simpson, *What is the Gospel?* Longmans. 2s. 6d. 1914.

*J. K. Mozley, *The Doctrine of the Atonement.* Duckworth. 2s. 6d. 1915.

G. B. Stevens. *The Christian Doctrine of Salvation.* T. & T. Clark. 12s. 1905.

W. P. DuBose, *The Gospel according to St. Paul.* Longmans. 5s. 1907.

In connexion herewith, for the Christian Doctrine of Man :—

H. W. Robinson, *The Christian Doctrine of Man.* T. & T. Clark. 6s. 1911.

H. V. S. Eck, *Sin.* Longmans. 5s. 1907.

F. J. Hall, *Evolution and the Fall.* Longmans. 5s. 1910.

F. R. Tennant, *The Origin and Propagation of Sin.* Camb. Univ. Press. 3s. 6d. 1902.

R. Mackintosh, *Christianity and Sin.* Duckworth. 2s. 6d. 1913.

*C. Gore, *The Permanent Creed and the Christian Idea of Sin.* Murray. 6d. 1905.

*A. Chandler, *The Spirit of Man.* Longmans. 5s. 1891.

VI

THE RESURRECTION OF JESUS CHRIST

T. J. Thorburn, *The Resurrection Narratives.* Kegan Paul. 6s. 1910.

J. Orr, *The Resurrection of Jesus.* Hodder & Stoughton. 6s. 1908.

W. J. Sparrow Simpson, *The Resurrection and Modern Thought.* Longmans. 7s. 6d. 1911.

W. J. Sparrow Simpson, *Our Lord's Resurrection.* Longmans. 5s. 1905.

*B. F. Westcott, *The Revelation of the Risen Lord.* Macmillan. 6s. 1881.

*W. Milligan. *The Resurrection of our Lord.* Macmillan. 5s. 1881.

H. B. Swete, *The Appearances of our Lord after His Passion.* Macmillan. 2s. 6d. 1907.

H. Latham, *The Risen Master.* Deighton Bell. 6s. 1900.

C. H. Robinson, *Studies in the Resurrection of Christ.* Longmans. 3s. 6d. 1909.

R. M. Benson, *The Life beyond the Grave.* Longmans. 5s. 1885.

VII

THE ASCENSION OF JESUS CHRIST

*H. B. Swete, *The Ascended Christ.* Macmillan. 2s. 6d. 1910.

*W. Milligan, *The Ascension and Heavenly Priesthood of our Lord.* Macmillan. 7s. 6d. 1892.

A. J. Tait, *The Heavenly Session of our Lord.* R. Scott. 6s. 1912.

B. F. Westcott, *The Epistle to the Hebrews.* Macmillan. 14s. 1889.

H. L. Martensen, *Christian Dogmatics.* Eng. tr. T. & T. Clark. 10s. 6d. 1866.

*B. F. Westcott, *The Revelation of the Risen Lord,* cc. X., XI. Macmillan. 6s. 1881.

VIII

JESUS CHRIST AS JUDGE

E. C. Dewick, *Primitive Christian Eschatology.* Camb. Univ. Press. 10s. 6d. 1912.

W. A. Brown, Arts. *Millennium* and *Parousia* in Hastings' *Dictionary of the Bible,* Vol. III. T. & T. Clark.

J. Langton Clarke, *The Eternal Saviour Judge.* Murray. 9s. 1905. Abridged edit. 1s.

*E. von Dobschütz, *The Eschatology of the Gospels.* Hodder & Stoughton. 5s. 1910.

Compare also some of the books under XIV.

IX

THE HOLY SPIRIT

*H. B. Swete, *The Holy Spirit in the New Testament.* Macmillan. 8s. 6d. 1909.

H. B. Swete, *The Holy Spirit in the Ancient Church.* Macmillan. 8s. 6d. 1912.

G. Moberly, *The Administration of the Holy Spirit.* Parker. 7s. 6d. 1882.

H. C. G. Moule, *Veni Creator.* Hodder & Stoughton. 5s. 1902.

A. B. Webb, *The Presence and Office of the Holy Spirit.* Skeffington. 3s. 6d. 1881.

W. H. Griffith Thomas, *The Holy Spirit of God.* Longmans. 6s. 1913.

J. H. B. Masterman, *I believe in the Holy Ghost.* Wells Gardner. 2s. 1906.

*T. Rees, *The Holy Spirit.* Duckworth. 2s. 6d. 1915.

A. C. Downer, *The Mission and Ministration of the Holy Spirit.* T. & T. Clark. 7s. 6d. 1909.

W. H. Hutchings, *The Person and Work of the Holy Ghost.* Longmans. 4th edit. 4s. 6d. 1893.

*W. L. Walker, *The Spirit and the Incarnation.* T. & T. Clark. 9s. 1899.

E. W. Winstanley, *Spirit in the New Testament.* Camb. Univ. Press. 3s. 6d. 1908.

C. Gore, Art. *The Holy Spirit and Inspiration* in *Lux Mundi.* Murray. 2s. 6d. 1889.

G. H. S. Walpole, *The Mission of the Holy Ghost.* Longmans. 2s. 1906.

G. F. Holden, *The Holy Ghost the Comforter.* Longmans. 4s. 6d. 1908.

X

THE HOLY TRINITY

C. F. D'Arcy, *Idealism and Theology : a Study of Presuppositions.* Hodder & Stoughton. 6s. 1899.

J. R. Illingworth, *The Doctrine of the Trinity.* Macmillan. 6s. 1907.

L. G. Mylne, *The Holy Trinity.* Longmans. 7s. 6d. 1915.

*F. J. Hall, *The Trinity.* Longmans. 6s. 1911.

*W. P. DuBose, *The Ecumenical Councils.* T. & T. Clark. 6s. 1896.

J. Lebreton, *Les Origines du Dogme de la Trinité.* Paris: Beauchesne. 8fr. 1910.

H. M. Scott, Art. *Trinity*, in the Extra volume of Hastings' *Dictionary of the Bible*. T. & T. Clark.

Help may also be obtained from a number of the books given under II and III.

XI

THE HOLY CATHOLIC CHURCH

F. D. Maurice, *The Kingdom of Christ.* 2 Vols. Rivington. 1842. Dent (*Everyman's Library*). 2 Vols. 1*s.* 3*d.* each.

F. J. A. Hort, *The Christian Ecclesia.* Macmillan. 6*s.* 1898.

J. B. Lightfoot, *The Christian Ministry.* Macmillan. 3*s.* 1901.

*C. Gore, *The Church and the Ministry.* Longmans. 6*s.* 1888.

C. Gore, *Orders and Unity.* Murray. 3*s.* 6*d.* 1909.

R. C. Moberly, *Ministerial Priesthood.* Murray. 6*s.* 1897.

*H. B. Swete, *The Holy Catholic Church: the Communion of Saints.* Macmillan. 3*s.* 6*d.* 1915.

*D. Stone, *The Christian Church.* Rivington. 7*s.* 6*d.* 1905.

D. Stone, *The Church: its Ministry and Authority.* Rivington. 1*s.* 1902.

T. M. Lindsay, *The Ministry in the Ancient Church.* Hodder & Stoughton. 10*s.* 6*d.* 1902. (Presbyterian.)

W. Lowrie, *The Church and its Organization in Primitive and Catholic Times.* Longmans. 14*s.* net. 1904.

W. Sanday, *The Conception of Priesthood.* Longmans. 3*s.* 6*d.* 1898.

W. Sanday, *The Primitive Church and Reunion.* Oxford Univ. Press. 1913. 4*s.* 6*d.*

A. E. J. Rawlinson, Art. *The Principle of Authority,* in *Foundations.* Macmillan. 10*s.* 6*d.* 1912.

D. Stone, *Holy Baptism.* Longmans. 5*s.* 1899.

J. B. Mozley, *The Primitive Doctrine of Baptismal Regeneration.* Murray. 7*s.* 6*d.* 1856.

F. H. Chase, *Confirmation in the Apostolic Age.* Macmillan. 2*s.* 6*d.* 1909.

A. J. Mason, *The Relation of Confirmation to Baptism.* Longmans. 7*s.* 6*d.* 1891.

D. Waterland, *True Doctrine of the Eucharist.* Oxford Univ. Press. 6*s.* 6*d.*

*C. Gore, *The Body of Christ.* Murray. 2*s.* 6*d.* 1901.

H. Wace, ed., *The Holy Communion*, Report of Fulham Conference. Longmans. 3s. 1900. (Out of print.)

P. N. Waggett, *The Holy Eucharist*. Murray. 3s. 6d. net. 1906.

J. Wordsworth, *The Holy Communion*. Longmans. 5s. 1910.

J. R. Milne, *The Doctrine and Practice of the Eucharist*. Longmans. 3s. 6d. 1895.

W. Spens, *Belief and Practice*, cc. IX.–XI. Longmans. 6s. 1915.

H. B. Swete, *Eucharistic Belief in the Second and Third Centuries*, in "Journal of Theological Studies," Vol. III. Jan. 1902. Oxford Univ. Press. 3s. 6d.

A. R. Whitham, *Holy Orders*. Longmans. 5s. 1903.

T. A. Lacey, *Marriage in Church and State*. R. Scott. 5s. 1912.

F. W. Puller, *The Anointing of the Sick*. S.P.C.K. 5s. 1904.

XII

THE COMMUNION OF SAINTS

A. J. Mason, *Purgatory, the State of the Faithful Departed, and Invocation of Saints*. Longmans. 3s. 1901.

J. Wordsworth, *The Invocation of Saints and the Twenty-Second Article*. S.P.C.K. 6d. 1908.

D. Stone, *The Invocation of Saints*. Longmans. 1s. 1909.

*E. Vacandard, *Études*. Vol. III. Paris. 1905.

*H. F. Stewart, *Doctrina Romanensium de Invocatione Sanctorum*. S.P.C.K. 2s. 6d. 1907.

J. P. Kirsch, *The Doctrine of the Communion of Saints in the Ancient Church*. Eng. tr. Sands. 5s. 1910.

H. B. Swete, *Prayer for the Departed in the First Four Centuries*, in "Journal of Theological Studies," Vol. VIII. July, 1907. Oxford Univ. Press. 3s. 6d.

*H. B. Swete, *The Holy Catholic Church: the Communion of Saints*. Macmillan. 3s. 6d.

A. J. Worlledge, *Prayer*. Longmans. 5s. 1902.

G. Tyrrell, *Lex Credendi*. Longmans. 5s. 1905.

C. Gore, *Prayer and the Lord's Prayer*. Wells Gardner. 6d. 1898.

B. H. Streeter, ed., *Concerning Prayer*. Macmillan. 7s. 6d. 1916.

XIII

THE FORGIVENESS OF SINS

*H. B. Swete, *The Forgiveness of Sins.* Macmillan. 2s. 6d. 1916.

H. B. Swete, *Penitential Discipline in the First Three Centuries,* in "Journal of Theological Studies," Vol. IV. April, 1903. Oxford Univ. Press. 3s. 6d.

H. Wace, ed., *Confession and Absolution.* Report of Fulham Conference. Longmans. 3s. 1902. (Out of print.)

T. W. Drury, *Confession and Absolution.* Hodder & Stoughton. 6s. 1904.

E. T. Churton, *The Use of Penitence.* Longmans. 6s. 1905.

Compare also the literature under V.

XIV

THE RESURRECTION OF THE BODY, THE LIFE EVERLASTING.

*S. D. F. Salmond, *The Christian Doctrine of Immortality.* T. & T. Clark. 9s. 1895.

S. C. Gayford, *The Future State.* Rivingtons. 1s. 6d. 1903. (Out of print.)

S. C. Gayford, *Life after Death.* Masters. 2s. 6d. 1909.

J. Agar Beet, *The Last Things.* Hodder & Stoughton. 6s. 1897.

H. N. Oxenham, *Catholic Eschatology and Universalism.* W. H. Allen. 7s. 6d. 1876.

E. B. Pusey, *What is of Faith as to Everlasting Punishment?* Parker. 3s. 6d. 1879.

*W. A. Brown, *The Christian Hope.* Duckworth. 2s. 6d. 1912.

W. O. E. Oesterley, *The Doctrine of the Last Things : Jewish and Christian.* Murray. 3s. 6d. 1908.

H. A. A. Kennedy, *St. Paul's Conception of the Last Things.* Hodder & Stoughton. 7s. 6d. 1905.

E. E. Holmes, *Immortality.* Longmans. 5s. 1909.

R. H. Charles, *Critical History of the Doctrine of a Future Life in Israel, in Judaism, and in Christianity.* Black. 15s. 1899.

J. Paterson Smyth, *The Gospel of the Hereafter.* Hodder & Stoughton. 2s. 6d. 1910.

A. E. Taylor, Art. *The Belief in Immortality,* in *The Faith and the War.* Macmillan. 5s. 1915.

PRINTED BY WILLIAM CLOWES AND SONS, LIMITED, LONDON AND BECCLES.